# AN EPIC CYCLE PRODUCTION
# ETERNITY
# KILL

AN EPIC CYCLE PRODUCTION

# ETERNITY KILL

**Story: Grant Calof & Eric Eisner**
**Script: Grant Calof**

**Artwork:**
**Part One: Siddharth Kotian**
**Part Two: Edison George**

Editors: Eric Eisner & Sharad Devarajan
Consulting Editors: Grant Calof, Jake Ryan
Lettering: Nilesh S. Mahadik
Production Managers: Usha Alagappan, Ashwin Pande

For Epic Cycle:
Eric Eisner • Jake Ryan • Evan Lesser • Will Jobe

For Liquid Comics:
Sharad Devarajan, CEO • Gotham Chopra, Partner • Suresh Seetharaman, President

For Dynamite Entertainment:
Nick Barrucci, President • Juan Collado, Chief Operating Officer • Joseph Rybandt, Editor
Josh Johnson, Creative Director • Rich Young, Director Business Development
Jason Ullmeyer, Senior Designer • Josh Green, Traffic Coordinator • Chris Caniano, Production Assistant

First Printing
ISBN-10: 1-60690-364-0
ISBN-13: 978-1-60690-364-3
10 9 8 7 6 5 4 3 2 1

DYNAMITE



LIQUID COMICS

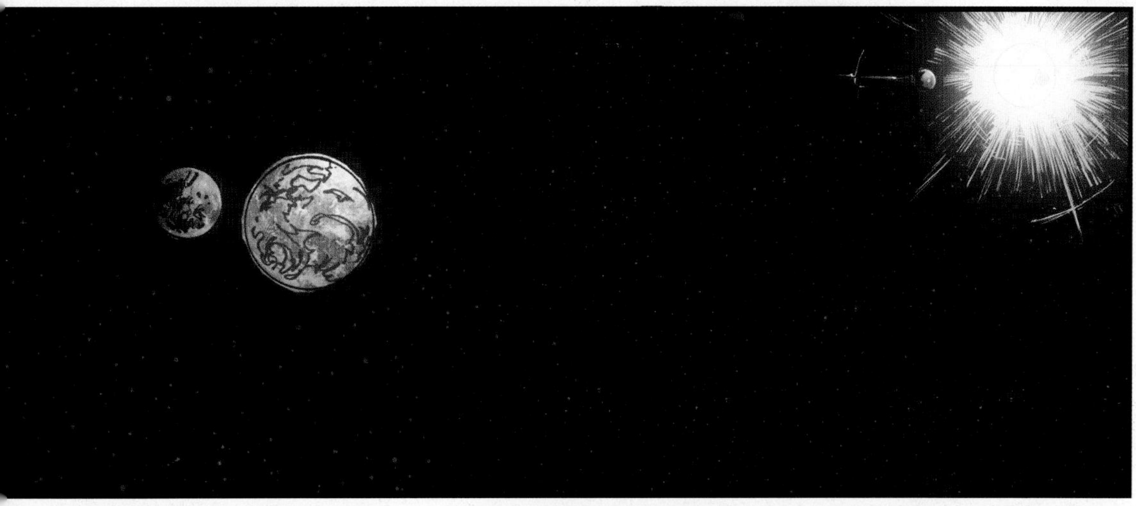

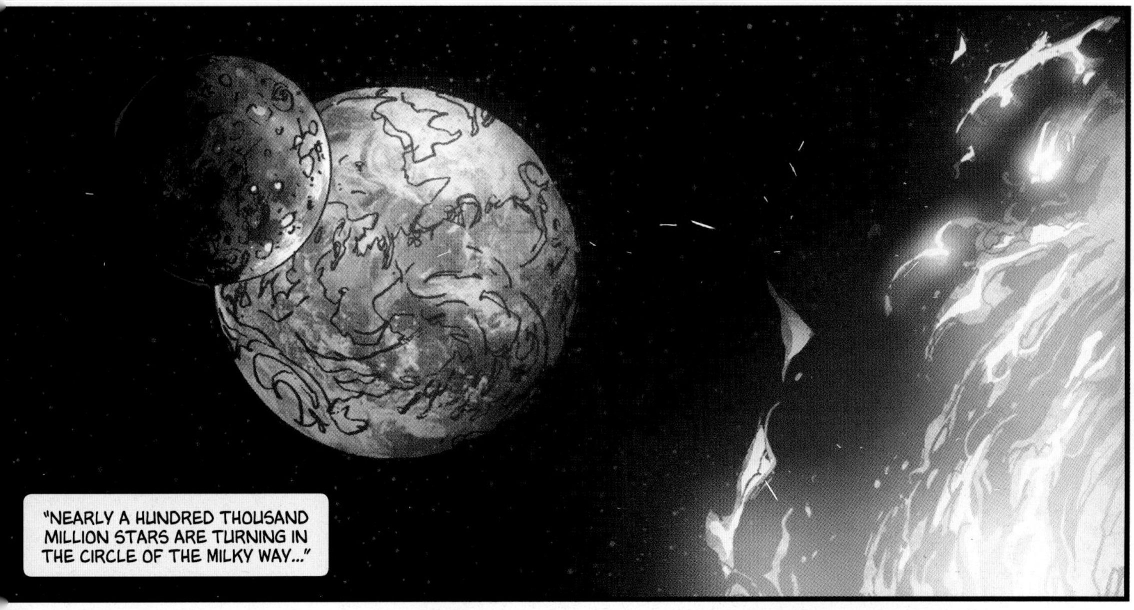
"NEARLY A HUNDRED THOUSAND MILLION STARS ARE TURNING IN THE CIRCLE OF THE MILKY WAY..."

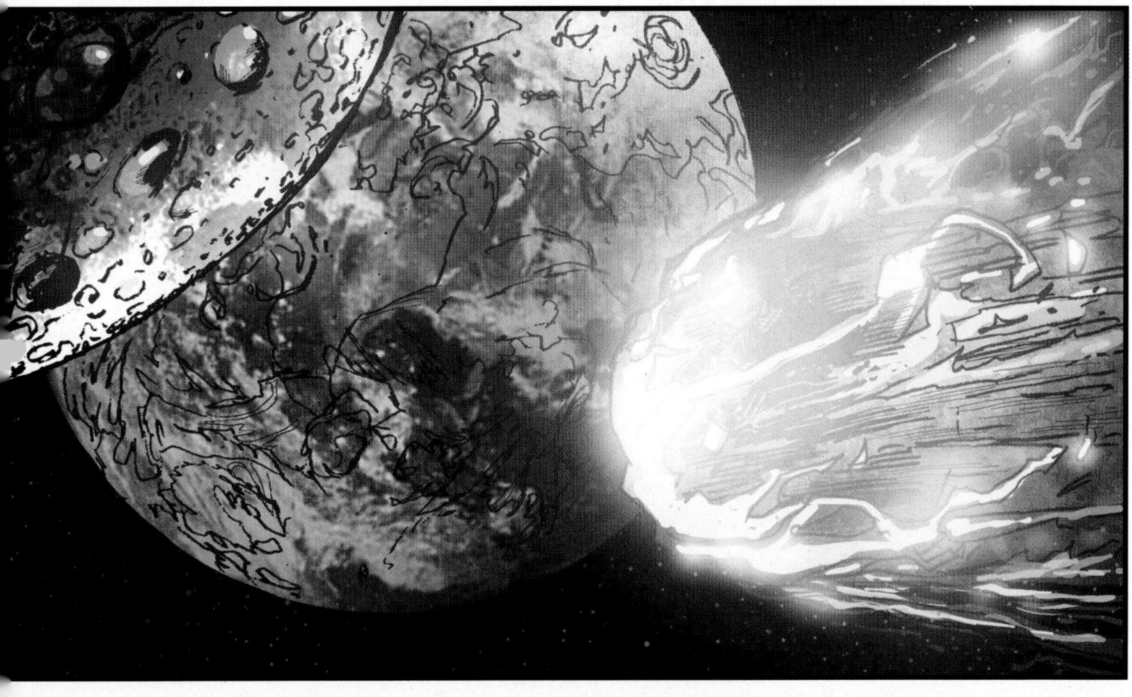

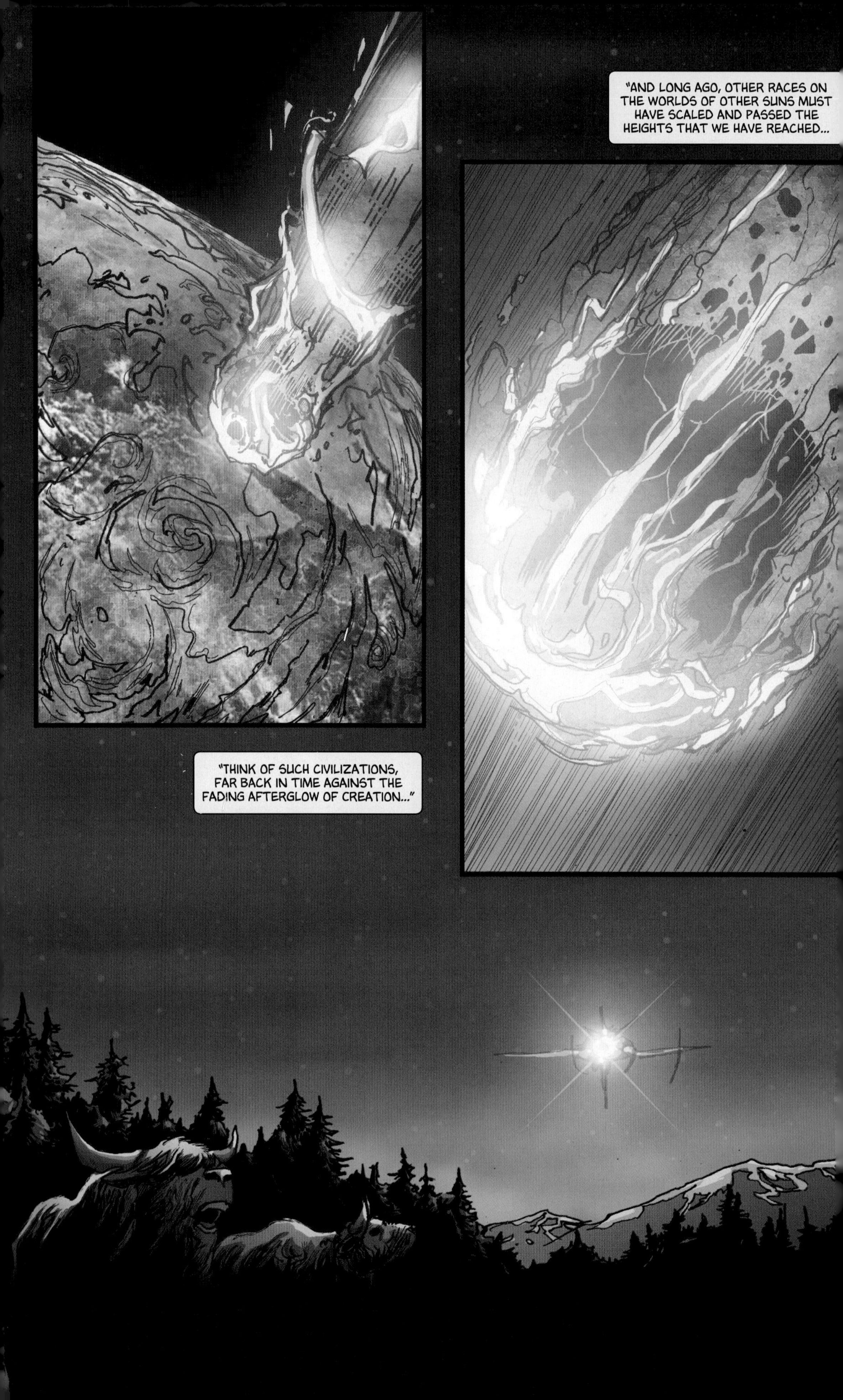
"AND LONG AGO, OTHER RACES ON THE WORLDS OF OTHER SUNS MUST HAVE SCALED AND PASSED THE HEIGHTS THAT WE HAVE REACHED...
"THINK OF SUCH CIVILIZATIONS, FAR BACK IN TIME AGAINST THE FADING AFTERGLOW OF CREATION..."

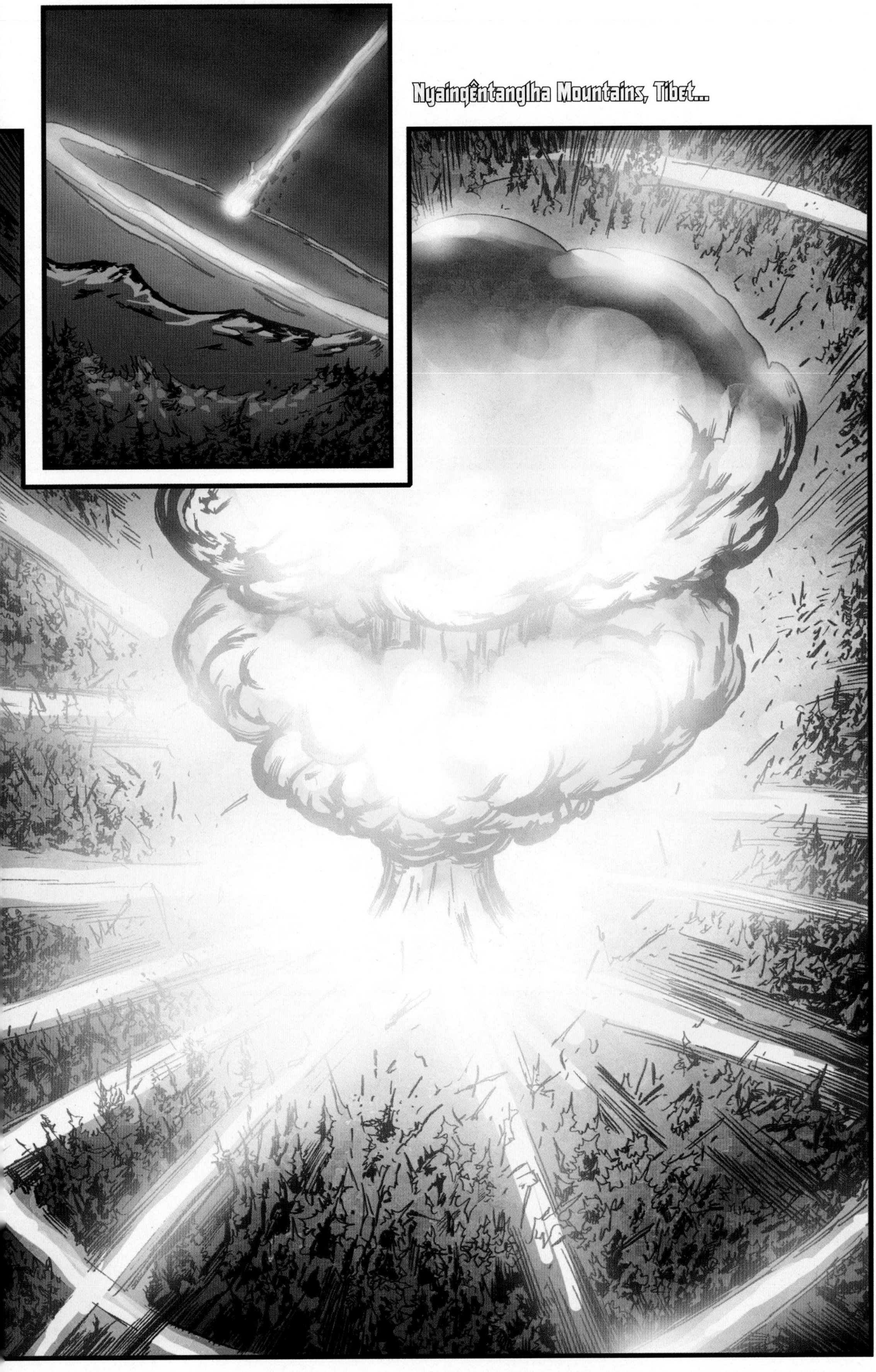
Nyainqêntanglha Mountains, Tibet...

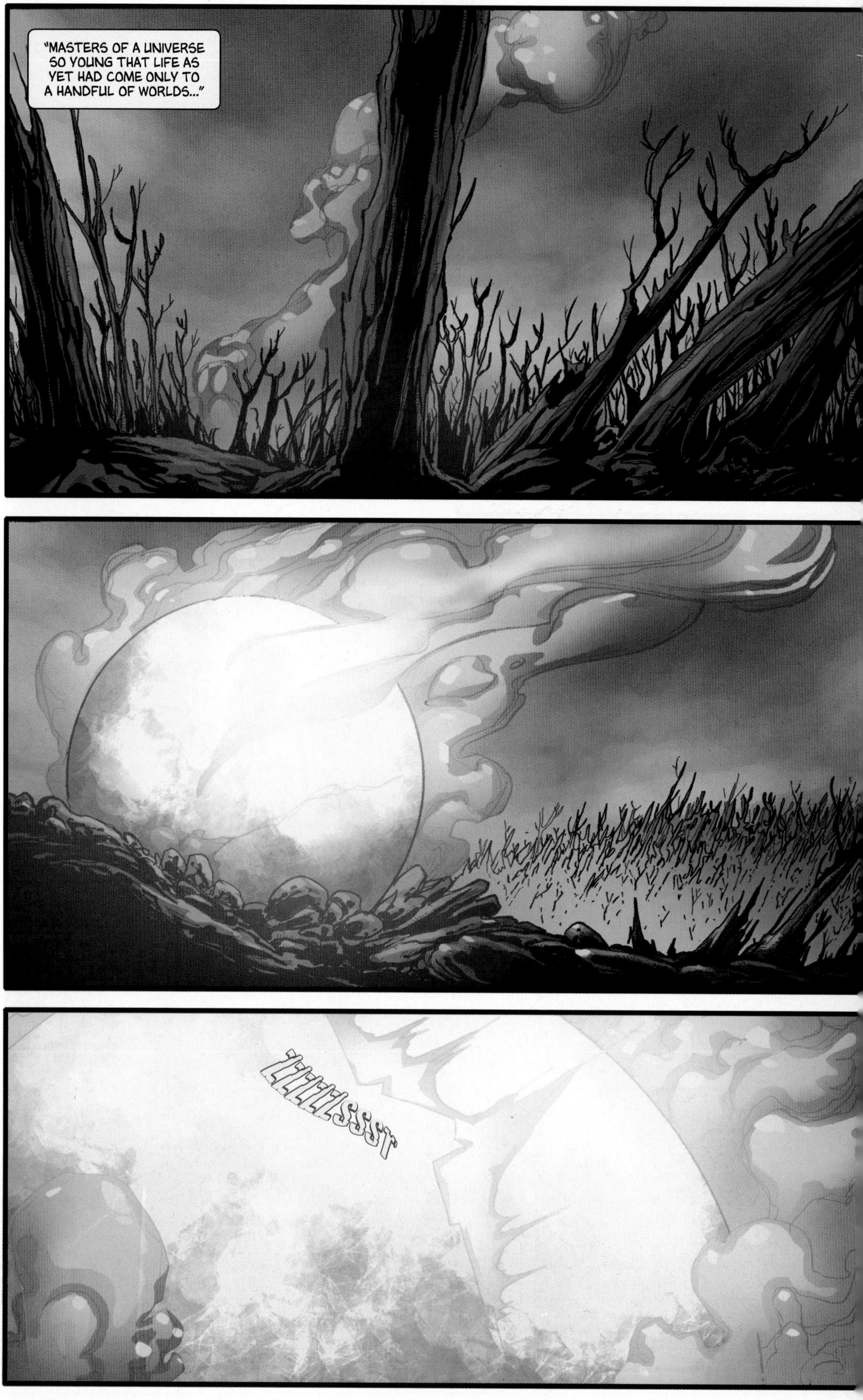
"MASTERS OF A UNIVERSE SO YOUNG THAT LIFE AS YET HAD COME ONLY TO A HANDFUL OF WORLDS..."
ZZZZZSSST

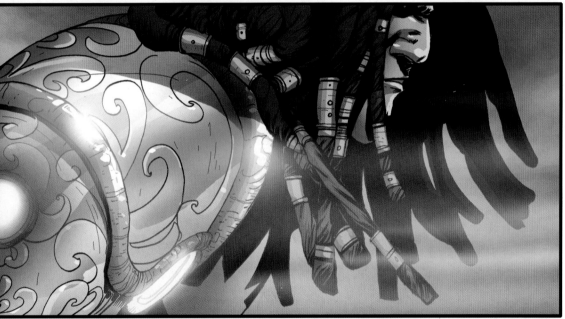

"THEIRS WOULD HAVE
BEEN A LONELINESS
WE CANNOT IMAGINE..."

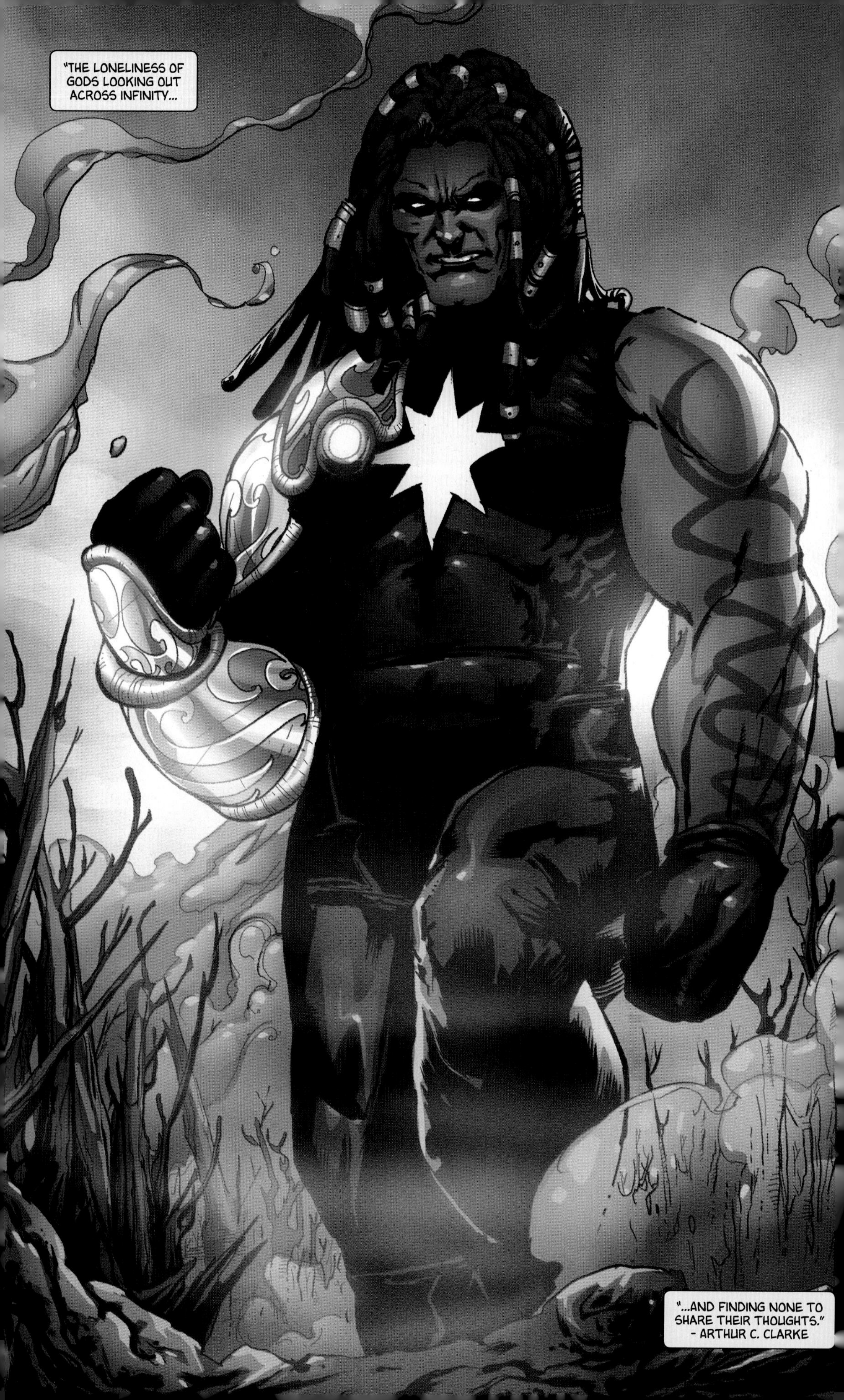
"THE LONELINESS OF GODS LOOKING OUT ACROSS INFINITY...
"...AND FINDING NONE TO SHARE THEIR THOUGHTS." - ARTHUR C. CLARKE

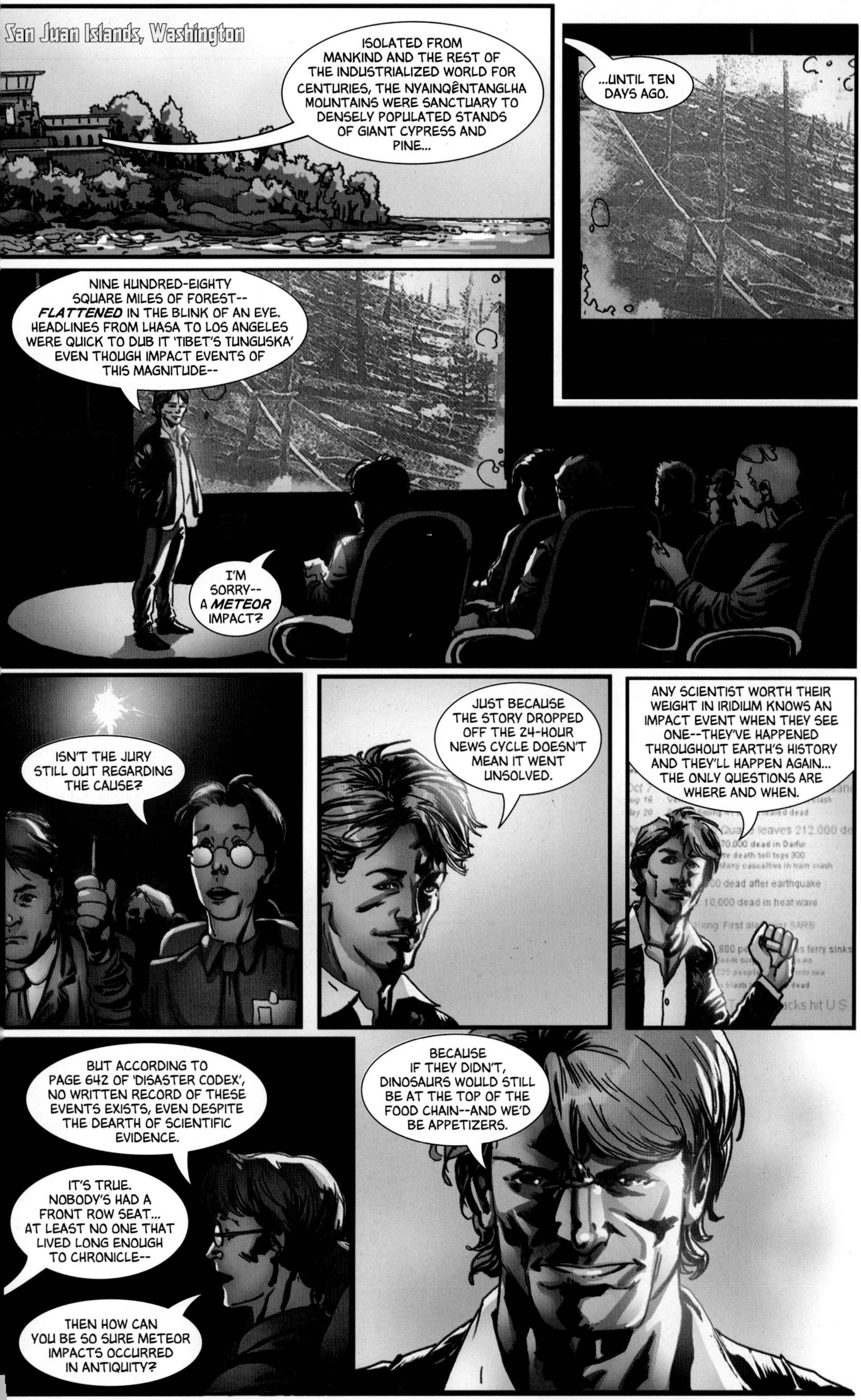
San Juan Islands, Washington
ISOLATED FROM MANKIND AND THE REST OF THE INDUSTRIALIZED WORLD FOR CENTURIES, THE NYAINQÊNTANGLHA MOUNTAINS WERE SANCTUARY TO DENSELY POPULATED STANDS OF GIANT CYPRESS AND PINE...
...UNTIL TEN DAYS AGO.
NINE HUNDRED-EIGHTY SQUARE MILES OF FOREST-- FLATTENED IN THE BLINK OF AN EYE. HEADLINES FROM LHASA TO LOS ANGELES WERE QUICK TO DUB IT 'TIBET'S TUNGUSKA' EVEN THOUGH IMPACT EVENTS OF THIS MAGNITUDE--
I'M SORRY-- A METEOR IMPACT?
ISN'T THE JURY STILL OUT REGARDING THE CAUSE?
JUST BECAUSE THE STORY DROPPED OFF THE 24-HOUR NEWS CYCLE DOESN'T MEAN IT WENT UNSOLVED.
ANY SCIENTIST WORTH THEIR WEIGHT IN IRIDIUM KNOWS AN IMPACT EVENT WHEN THEY SEE ONE--THEY'VE HAPPENED THROUGHOUT EARTH'S HISTORY AND THEY'LL HAPPEN AGAIN... THE ONLY QUESTIONS ARE WHERE AND WHEN.
BUT ACCORDING TO PAGE 642 OF 'DISASTER CODEX', NO WRITTEN RECORD OF THESE EVENTS EXISTS, EVEN DESPITE THE DEARTH OF SCIENTIFIC EVIDENCE.
IT'S TRUE. NOBODY'S HAD A FRONT ROW SEAT... AT LEAST NO ONE THAT LIVED LONG ENOUGH TO CHRONICLE--
THEN HOW CAN YOU BE SO SURE METEOR IMPACTS OCCURRED IN ANTIQUITY?
BECAUSE IF THEY DIDN'T, DINOSAURS WOULD STILL BE AT THE TOP OF THE FOOD CHAIN--AND WE'D BE APPETIZERS.

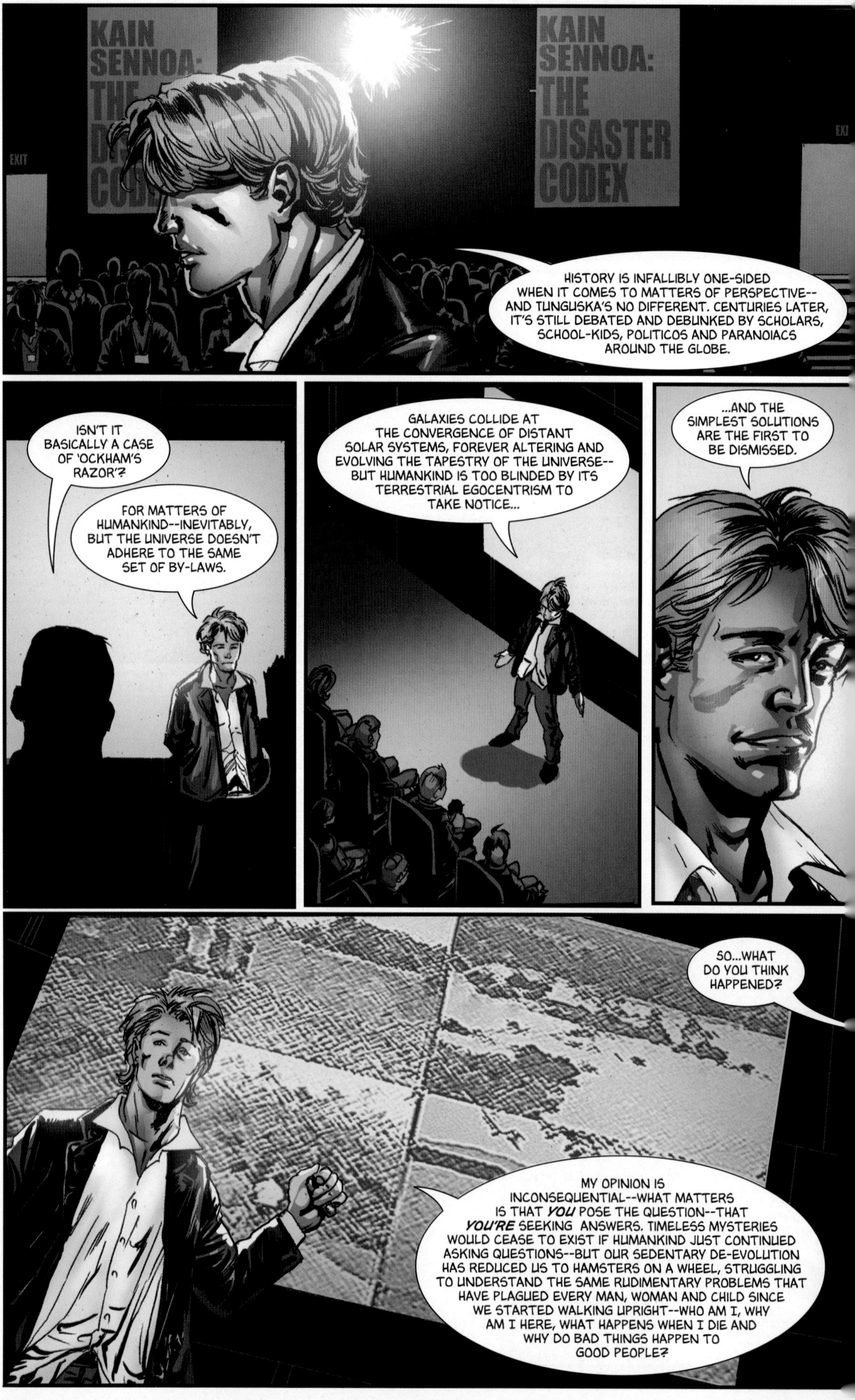
KAIN SENNOA: THE DISASTER CODEX
EXIT
HISTORY IS INFALLIBLY ONE-SIDED WHEN IT COMES TO MATTERS OF PERSPECTIVE--AND TUNGUSKA'S NO DIFFERENT. CENTURIES LATER, IT'S STILL DEBATED AND DEBUNKED BY SCHOLARS, SCHOOL-KIDS, POLITICOS AND PARANOIACS AROUND THE GLOBE.
ISN'T IT BASICALLY A CASE OF 'OCKHAM'S RAZOR'?
FOR MATTERS OF HUMANKIND--INEVITABLY, BUT THE UNIVERSE DOESN'T ADHERE TO THE SAME SET OF BY-LAWS.
GALAXIES COLLIDE AT THE CONVERGENCE OF DISTANT SOLAR SYSTEMS, FOREVER ALTERING AND EVOLVING THE TAPESTRY OF THE UNIVERSE--BUT HUMANKIND IS TOO BLINDED BY ITS TERRESTRIAL EGOCENTRISM TO TAKE NOTICE...
...AND THE SIMPLEST SOLUTIONS ARE THE FIRST TO BE DISMISSED.
SO...WHAT DO YOU THINK HAPPENED?
MY OPINION IS INCONSEQUENTIAL--WHAT MATTERS IS THAT YOU POSE THE QUESTION--THAT YOU'RE SEEKING ANSWERS. TIMELESS MYSTERIES WOULD CEASE TO EXIST IF HUMANKIND JUST CONTINUED ASKING QUESTIONS--BUT OUR SEDENTARY DE-EVOLUTION HAS REDUCED US TO HAMSTERS ON A WHEEL, STRUGGLING TO UNDERSTAND THE SAME RUDIMENTARY PROBLEMS THAT HAVE PLAGUED EVERY MAN, WOMAN AND CHILD SINCE WE STARTED WALKING UPRIGHT--WHO AM I, WHY AM I HERE, WHAT HAPPENS WHEN I DIE AND WHY DO BAD THINGS HAPPEN TO GOOD PEOPLE?

DISSATISFIED WITH LONG-ACCEPTED TEXTBOOK TRIPE, I SOUGHT A NEW PARADIGM OF CRITICAL THINKING WITH ONE CORE TENET--THAT LIKE THE TIDES, PATTERNS EXIST AT ALL LEVELS OF LIFE IF WE LOOK CLOSELY ENOUGH. BE IT BIRCH LEAVES, LIGHTHOUSES, FINGERPRINTS, FREEWAYS, TWENTIETH CENTURY TEMPLE-BUILDING OR NATURAL DISASTERS.

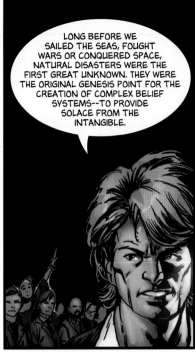

LONG BEFORE WE SAILED THE SEAS, FOUGHT WARS OR CONQUERED SPACE, NATURAL DISASTERS WERE THE FIRST GREAT UNKNOWN. THEY WERE THE ORIGINAL GENESIS POINT FOR THE CREATION OF COMPLEX BELIEF SYSTEMS--TO PROVIDE SOLACE FROM THE INTANGIBLE.

COMPARTMENTALIZED IN A MICROCOSM, EVEN THE MOST BRILLIANT MIND WOULD SEE ONLY A CHAOTIC STRING OF DISCONNECTED, COLOSSAL TRAGEDIES--BUT TO THE EXCOGITATED EYE, A SUBLIME PATTERN IS DETECTABLE.

A PATTERN SO VAST, IT TRANSCENDS COINCIDENCE INTO SYNCHRONICITY...PERHAPS EVEN TO AN ACT OF DIVINITY.

AN INTRIGUING PERSPECTIVE--PROVIDED YOU DEFINE THEOLOGY AND THEORETICAL SCIENCE EQUANIMOUSLY.

LET ME GUESS--FATALIST OR ATHEIST?

TRY PRAGMATIST.

...AND YET YOU STILL READ MY BOOKS?

ONLY TO HELP ME FALL ASLEEP.

HA HA HA

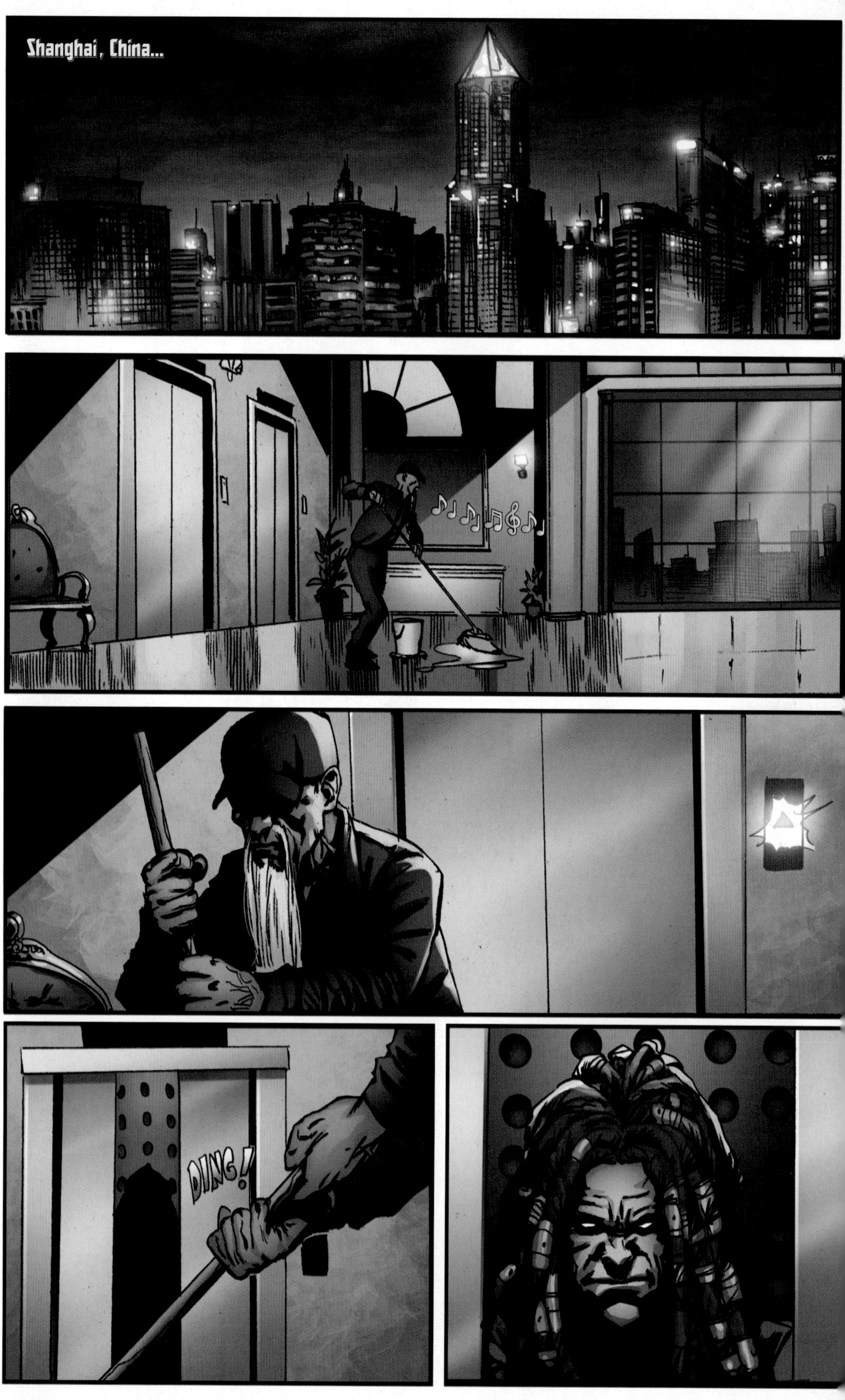
Shanghai, China...
DING!

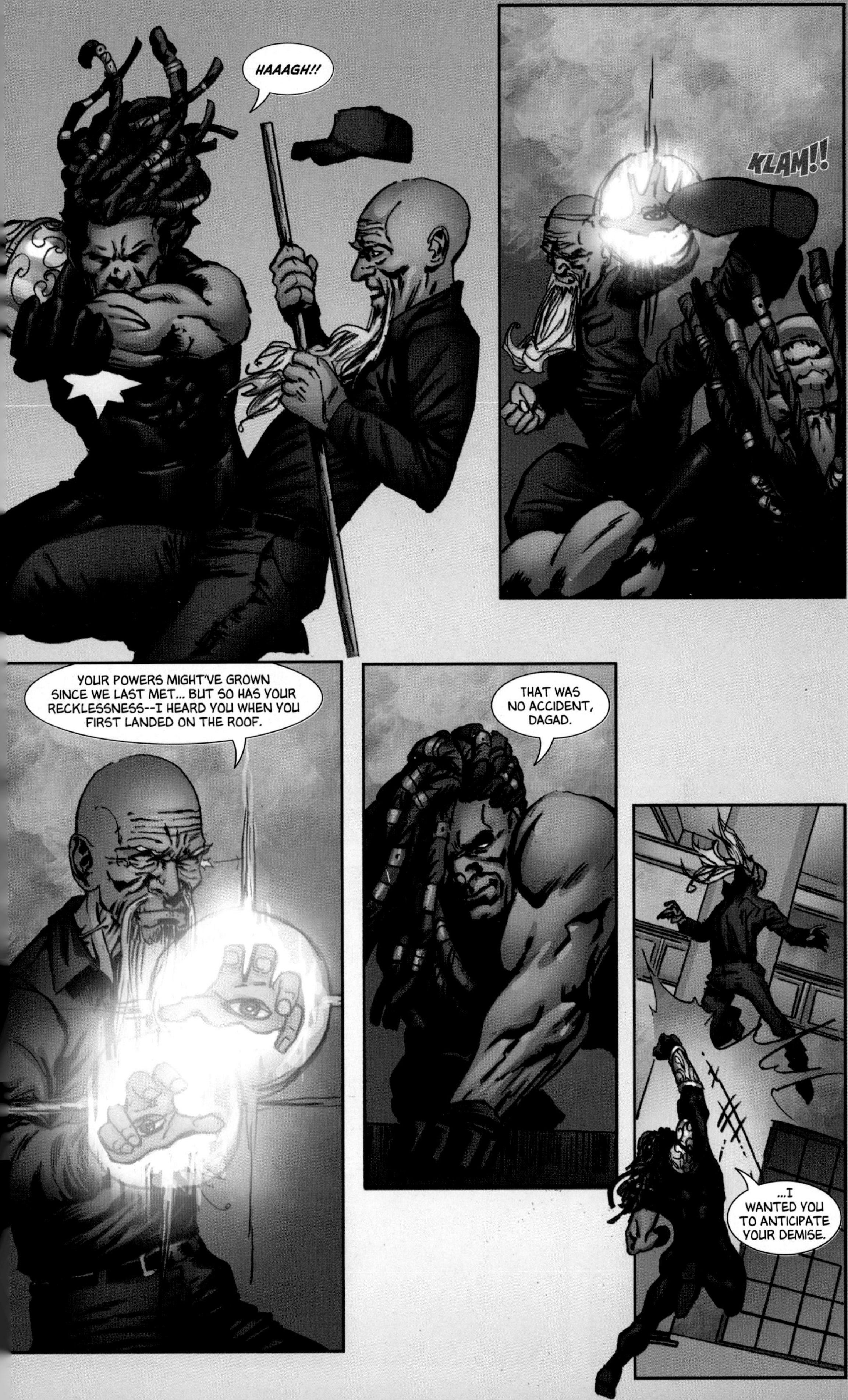
HAAAGH!!
KLAM!!
YOUR POWERS MIGHT'VE GROWN SINCE WE LAST MET... BUT SO HAS YOUR RECKLESSNESS--I HEARD YOU WHEN YOU FIRST LANDED ON THE ROOF.
THAT WAS NO ACCIDENT, DAGAD.
...I WANTED YOU TO ANTICIPATE YOUR DEMISE.

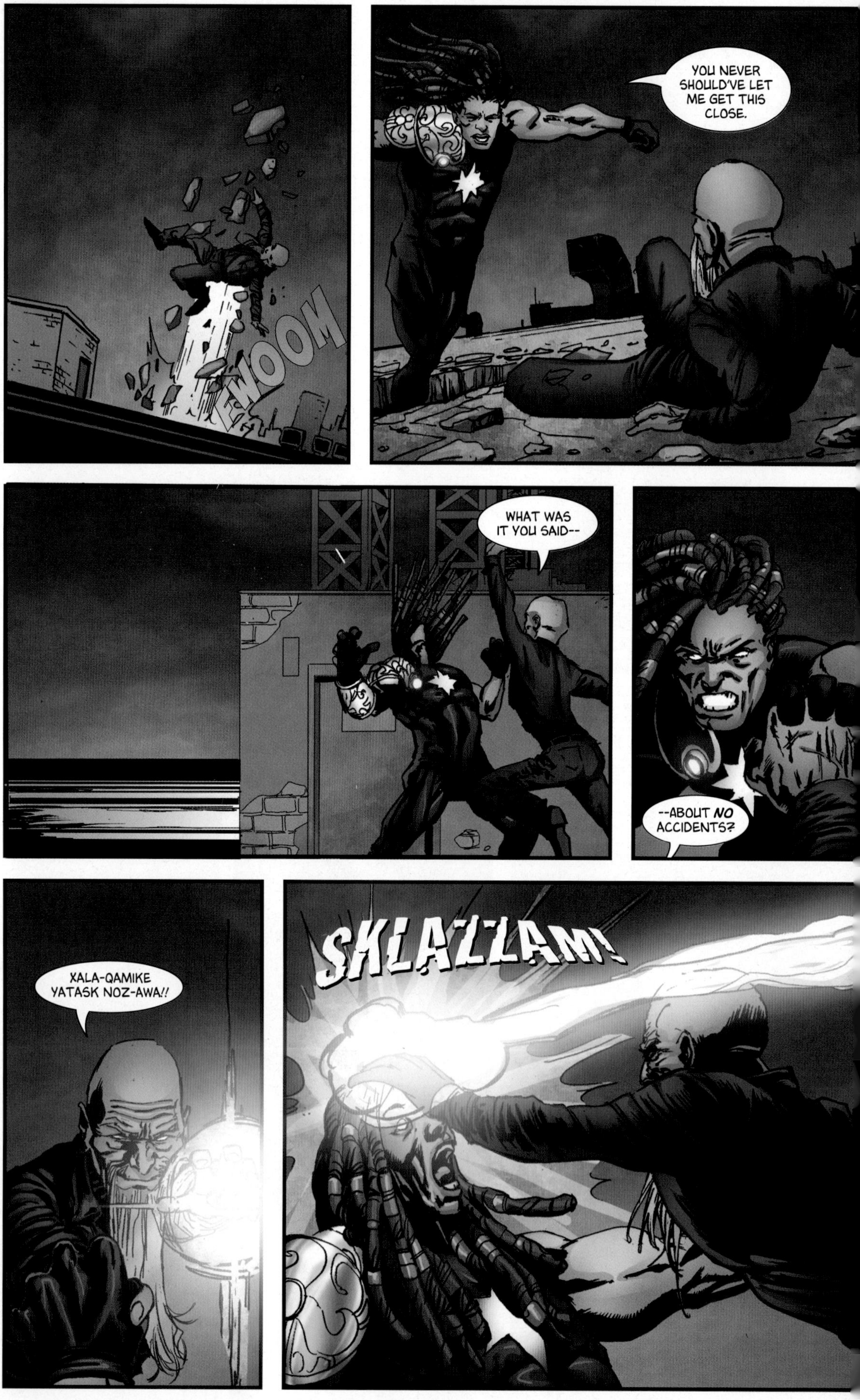
FWOOM
YOU NEVER SHOULD'VE LET ME GET THIS CLOSE.
WHAT WAS IT YOU SAID--
--ABOUT **NO** ACCIDENTS?
XALA-QAMIKE YATASK NOZ-AWA!!
SKLAZZAM!

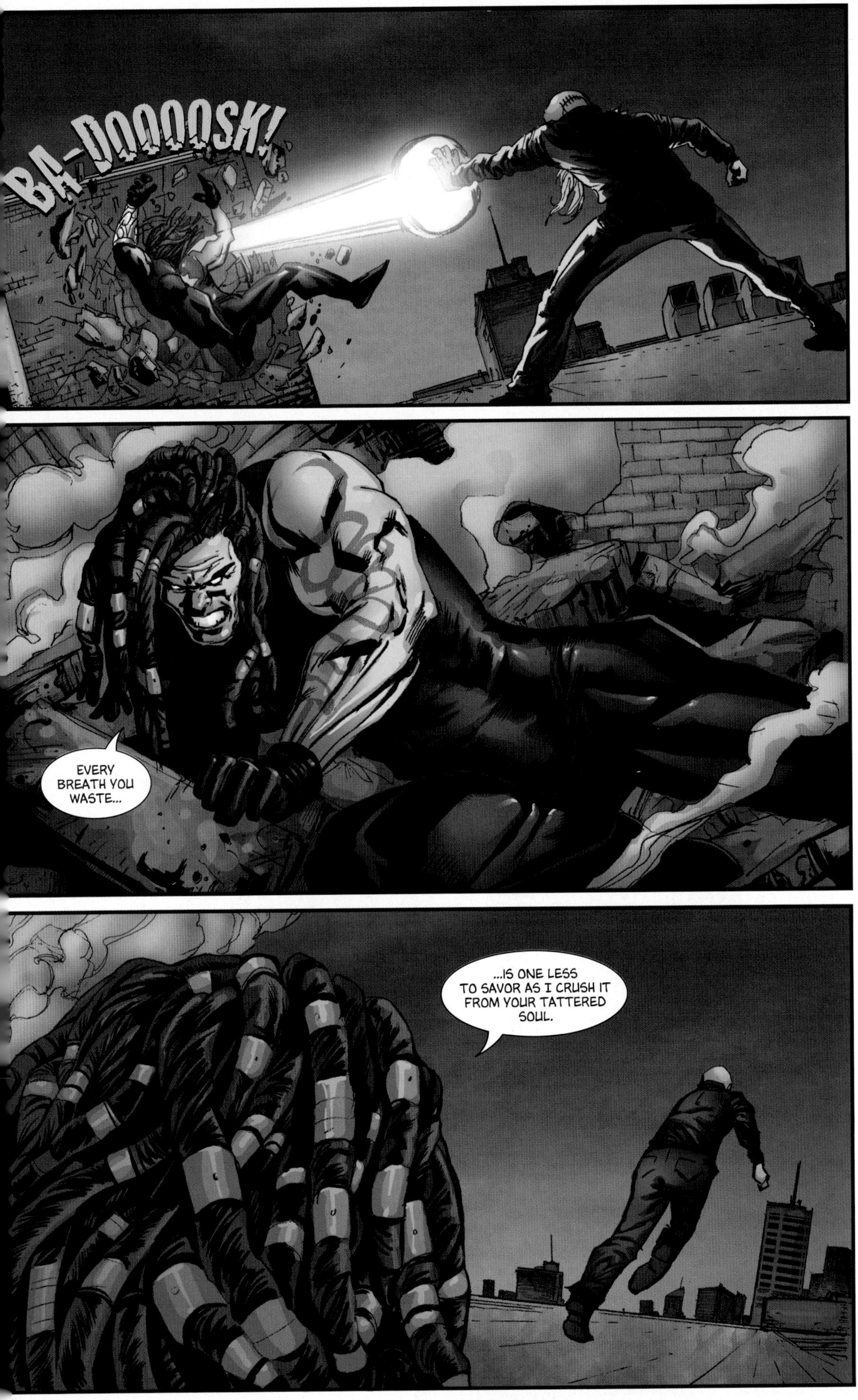
BA-DOOOOSK!
EVERY BREATH YOU WASTE...
...IS ONE LESS TO SAVOR AS I CRUSH IT FROM YOUR TATTERED SOUL.

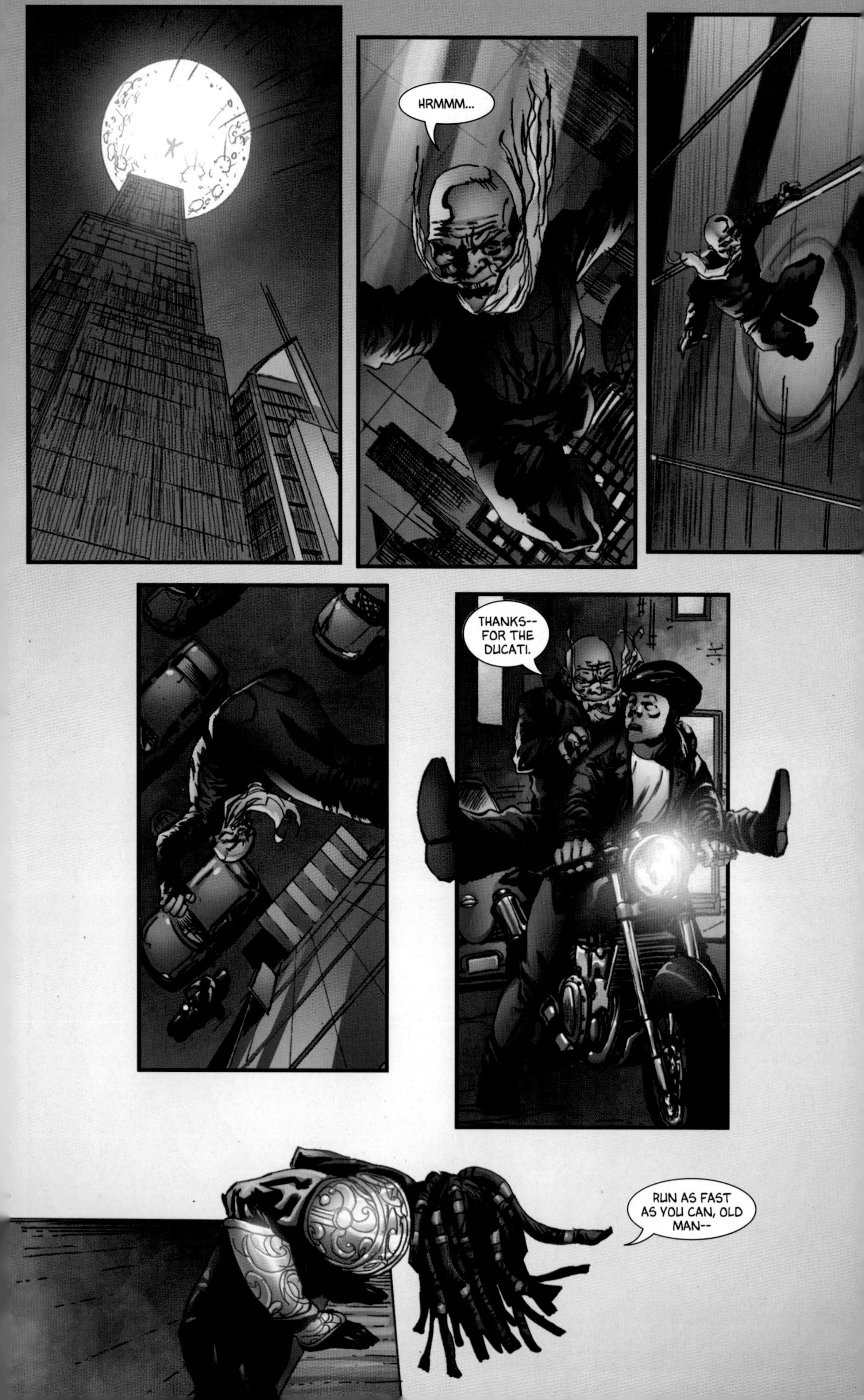
HRMMM...
THANKS-- FOR THE DUCATI.
RUN AS FAST AS YOU CAN, OLD MAN--

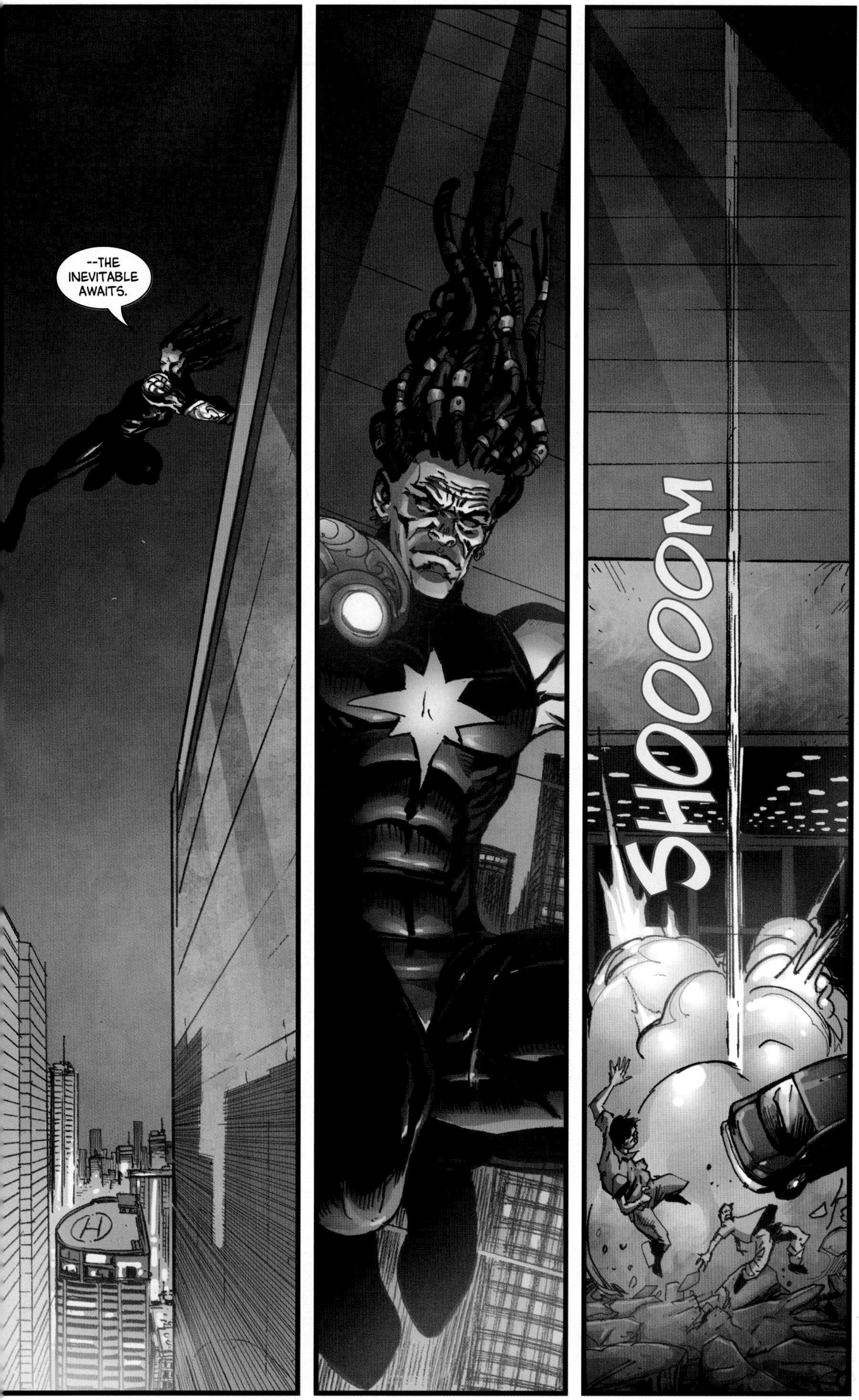
--THE INEVITABLE AWAITS.
SHOOOOM

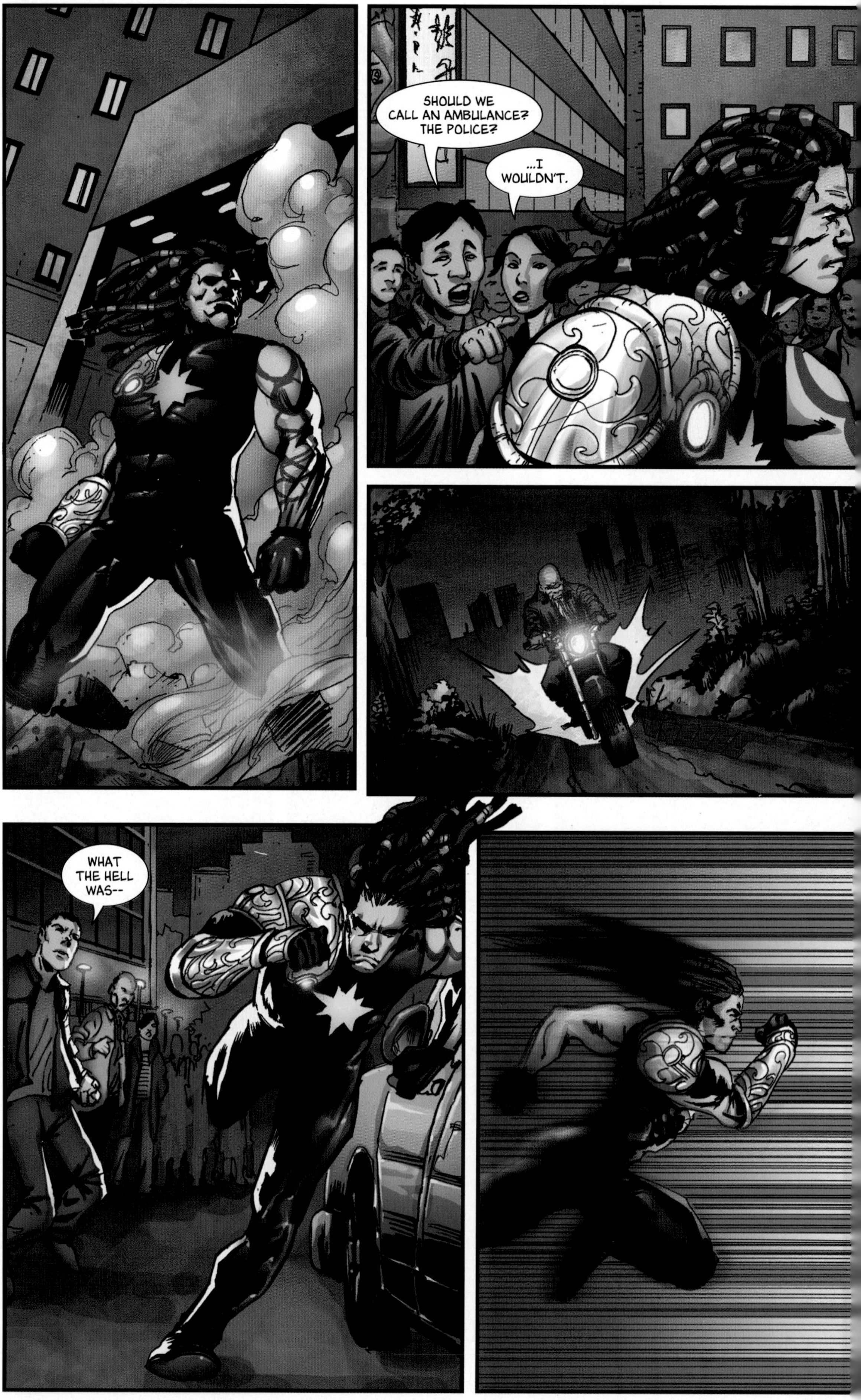
SHOULD WE CALL AN AMBULANCE? THE POLICE?
...I WOULDN'T.
WHAT THE HELL WAS--

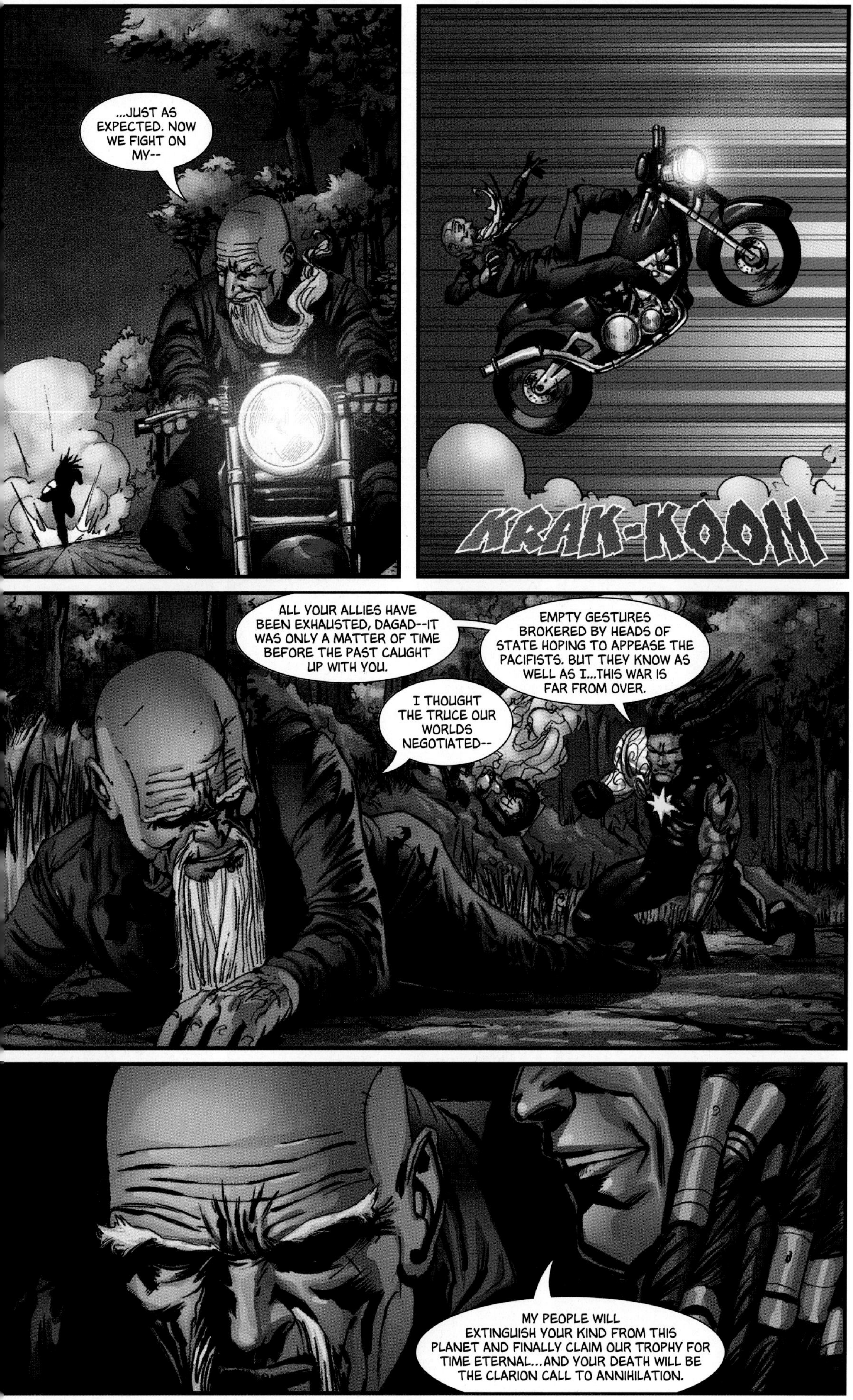
...JUST AS EXPECTED. NOW WE FIGHT ON MY--
KRAK-KOOM
ALL YOUR ALLIES HAVE BEEN EXHAUSTED, DAGAD--IT WAS ONLY A MATTER OF TIME BEFORE THE PAST CAUGHT UP WITH YOU.
I THOUGHT THE TRUCE OUR WORLDS NEGOTIATED--
EMPTY GESTURES BROKERED BY HEADS OF STATE HOPING TO APPEASE THE PACIFISTS. BUT THEY KNOW AS WELL AS I...THIS WAR IS FAR FROM OVER.
MY PEOPLE WILL EXTINGUISH YOUR KIND FROM THIS PLANET AND FINALLY CLAIM OUR TROPHY FOR TIME ETERNAL...AND YOUR DEATH WILL BE THE CLARION CALL TO ANNIHILATION.

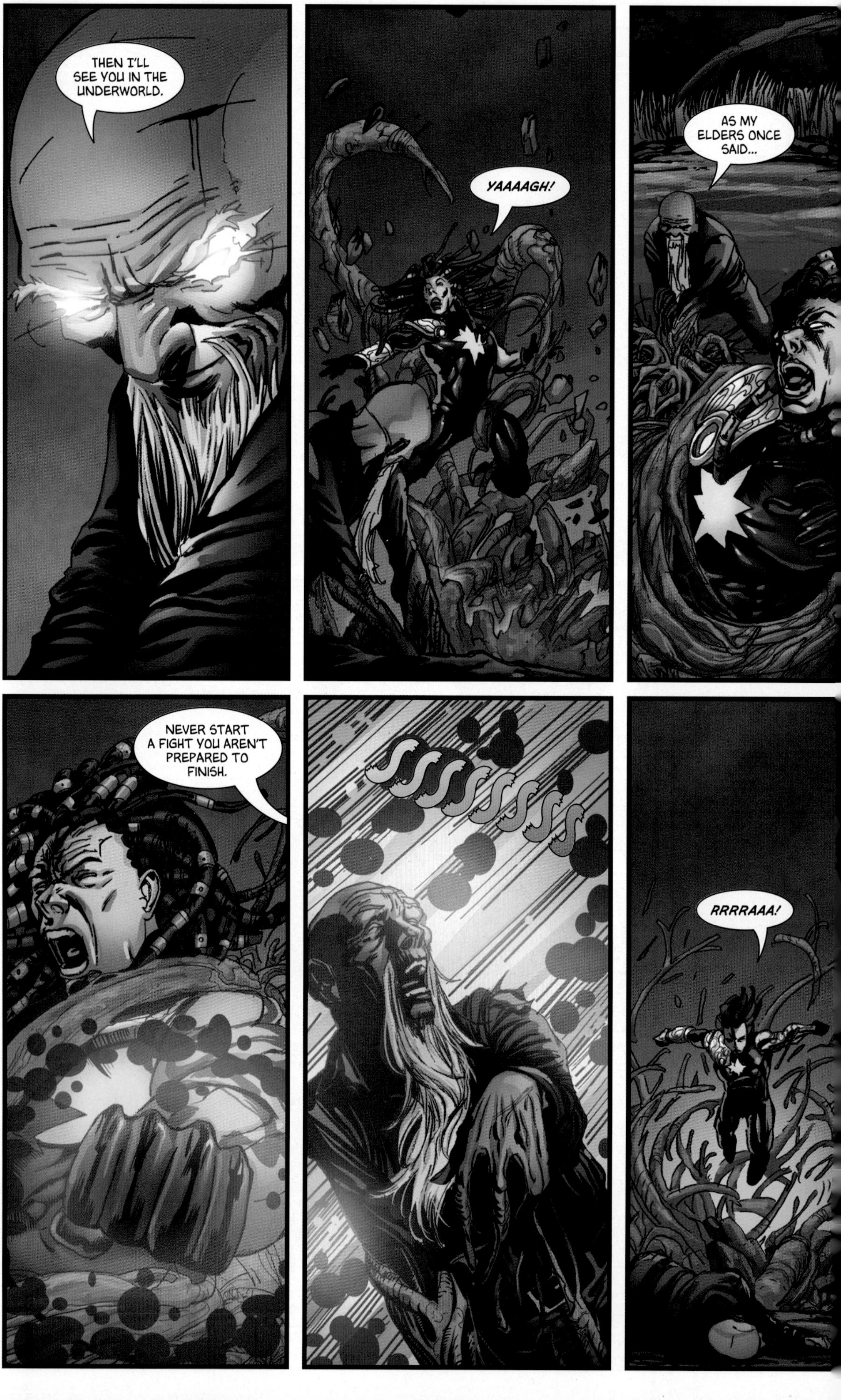
THEN I'LL SEE YOU IN THE UNDERWORLD.
YAAAAGH!
AS MY ELDERS ONCE SAID...
NEVER START A FIGHT YOU AREN'T PREPARED TO FINISH.
RRRRAAA!

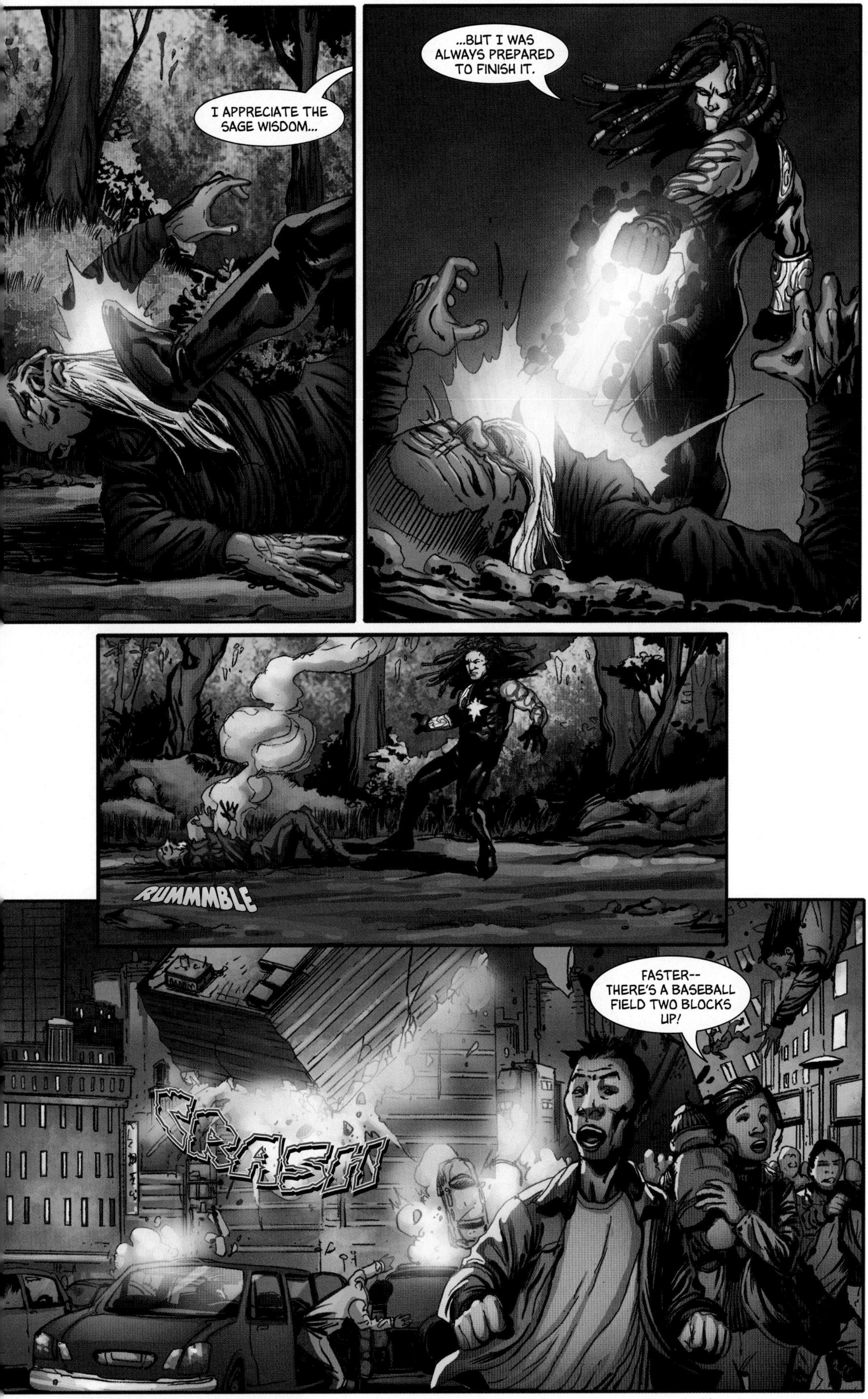
I APPRECIATE THE SAGE WISDOM...
...BUT I WAS ALWAYS PREPARED TO FINISH IT.
RUMMMBLE
CRASH
FASTER-- THERE'S A BASEBALL FIELD TWO BLOCKS UP!

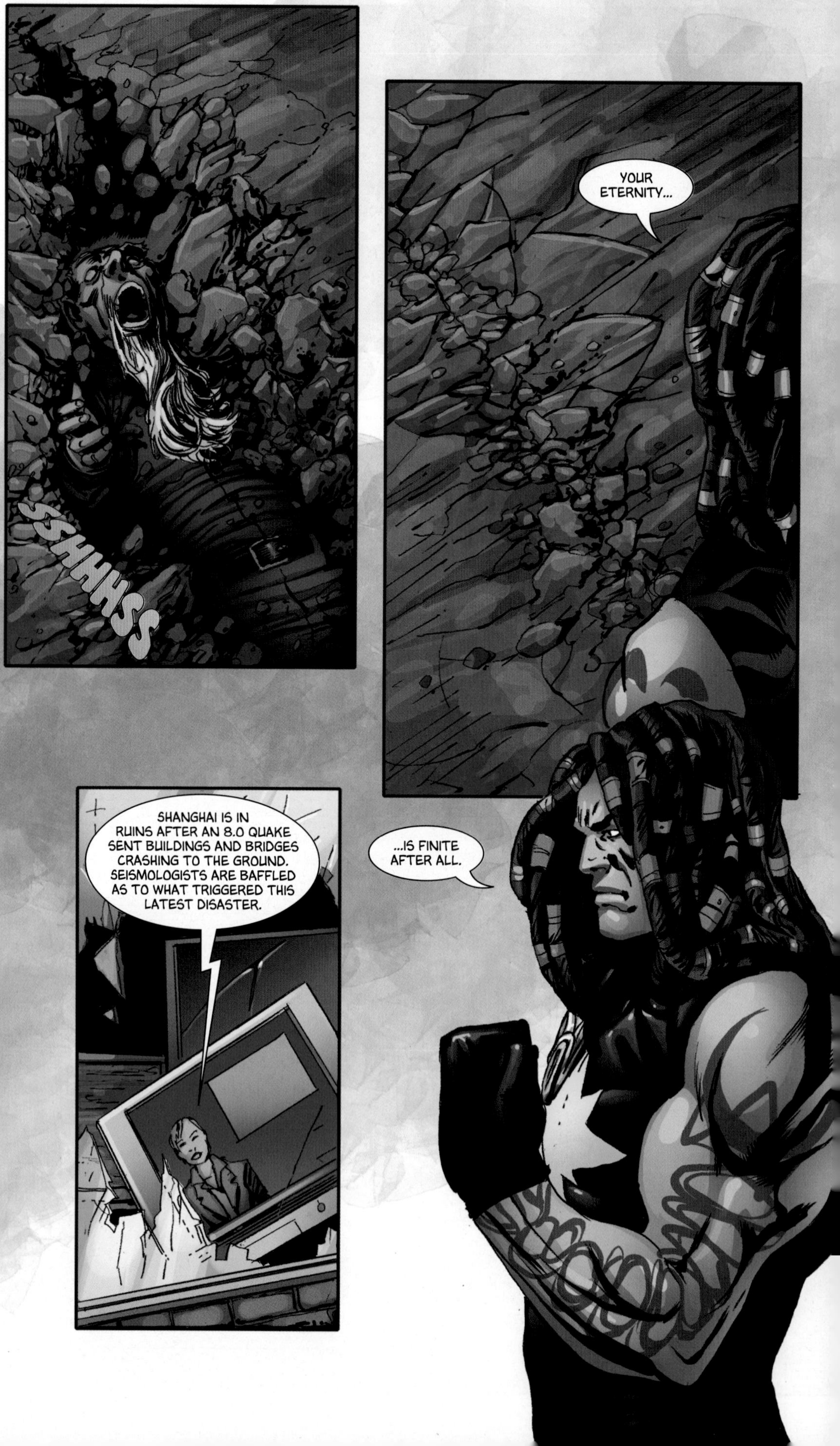
SSHHSS
YOUR ETERNITY...
SHANGHAI IS IN RUINS AFTER AN 8.0 QUAKE SENT BUILDINGS AND BRIDGES CRASHING TO THE GROUND. SEISMOLOGISTS ARE BAFFLED AS TO WHAT TRIGGERED THIS LATEST DISASTER.
...IS FINITE AFTER ALL.

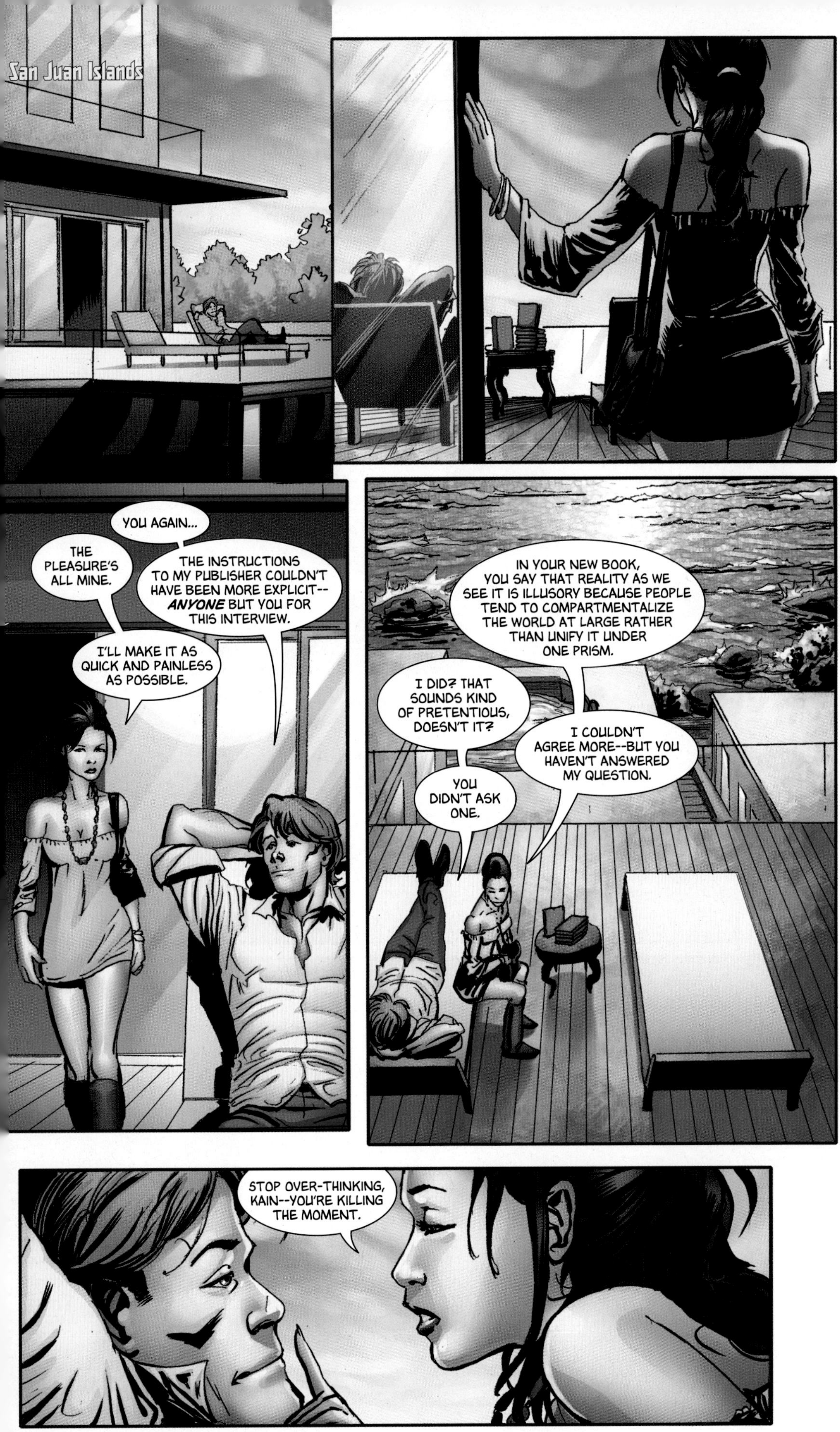
San Juan Islands
YOU AGAIN...
THE PLEASURE'S ALL MINE.
THE INSTRUCTIONS TO MY PUBLISHER COULDN'T HAVE BEEN MORE EXPLICIT-- ***ANYONE*** BUT YOU FOR THIS INTERVIEW.
I'LL MAKE IT AS QUICK AND PAINLESS AS POSSIBLE.
IN YOUR NEW BOOK, YOU SAY THAT REALITY AS WE SEE IT IS ILLUSORY BECAUSE PEOPLE TEND TO COMPARTMENTALIZE THE WORLD AT LARGE RATHER THAN UNIFY IT UNDER ONE PRISM.
I DID? THAT SOUNDS KIND OF PRETENTIOUS, DOESN'T IT?
I COULDN'T AGREE MORE--BUT YOU HAVEN'T ANSWERED MY QUESTION.
YOU DIDN'T ASK ONE.
STOP OVER-THINKING, KAIN--YOU'RE KILLING THE MOMENT.

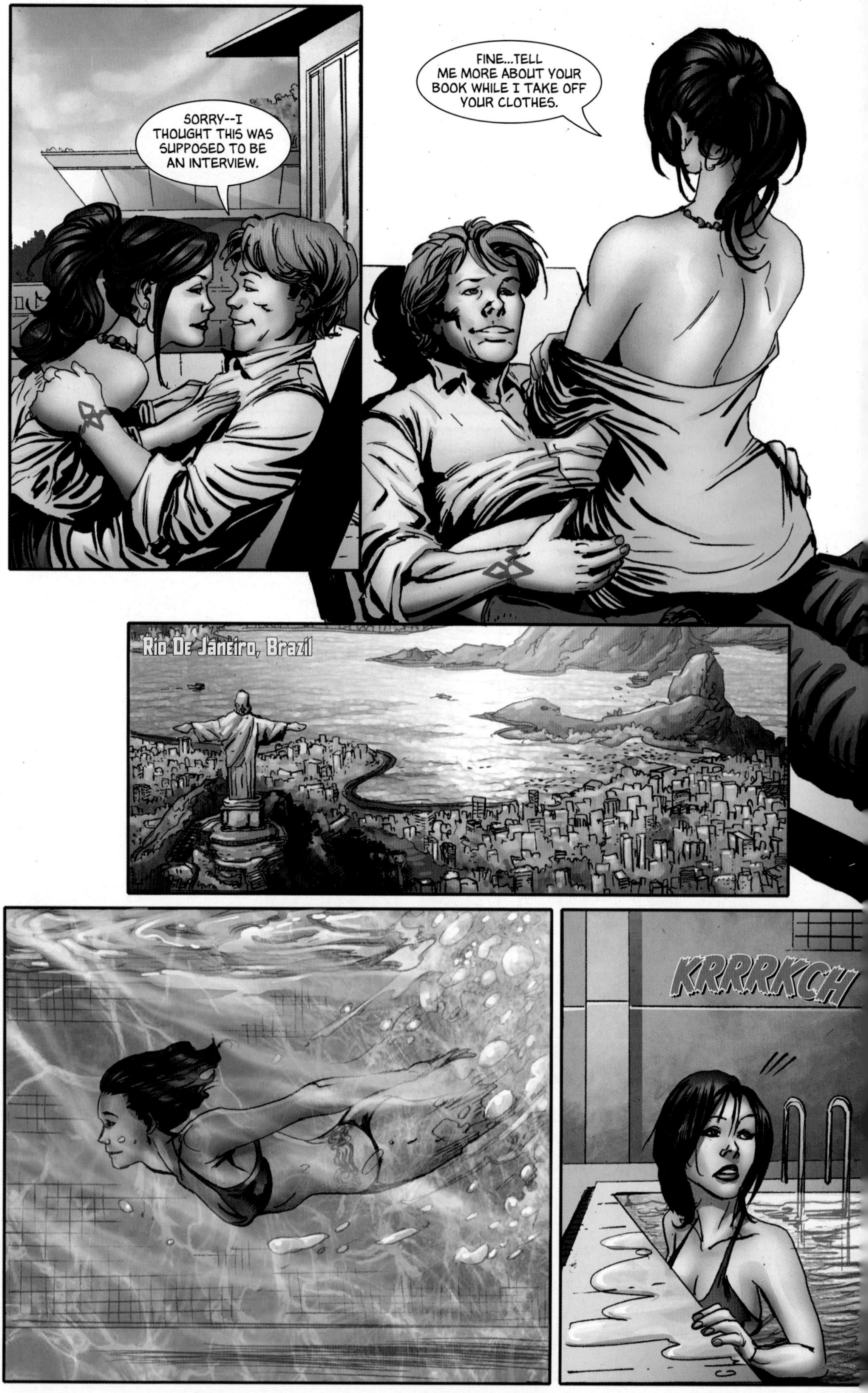
SORRY--I THOUGHT THIS WAS SUPPOSED TO BE AN INTERVIEW.
FINE...TELL ME MORE ABOUT YOUR BOOK WHILE I TAKE OFF YOUR CLOTHES.
Rio De Janeiro, Brazil
KRRRKCH

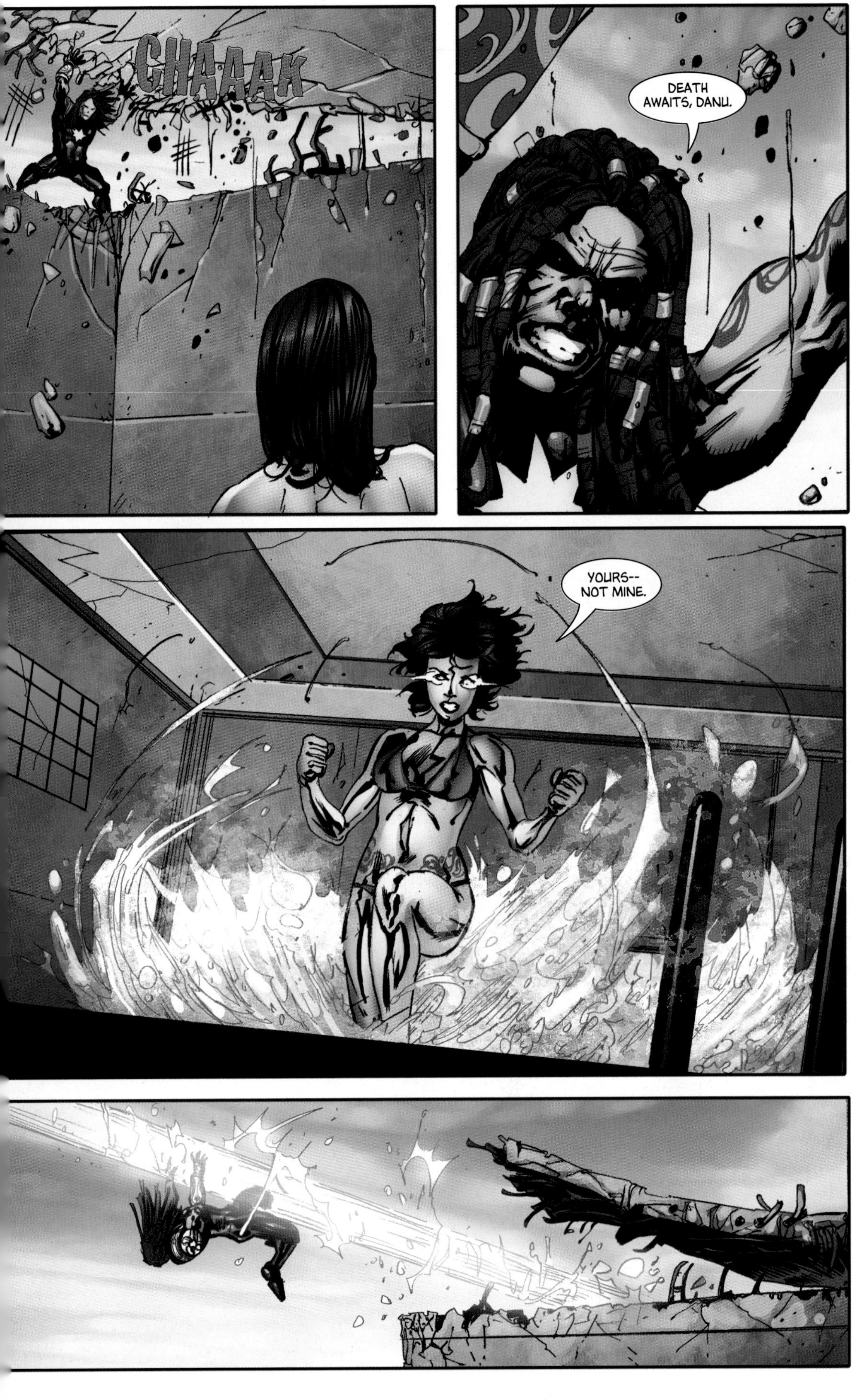
CHAAAK
DEATH AWAITS, DANU.
YOURS-- NOT MINE.

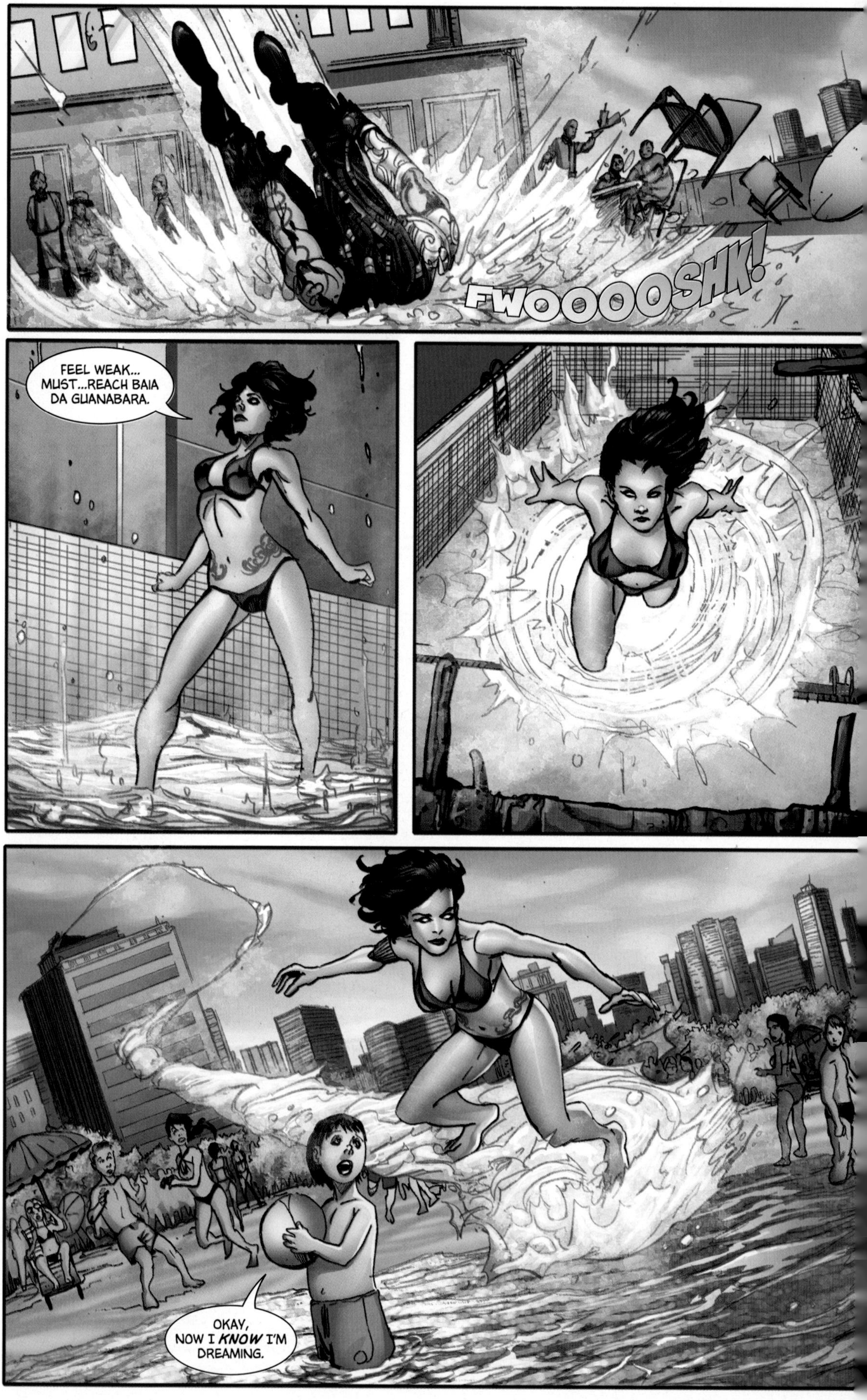
FWOOOOOSHK!
FEEL WEAK... MUST...REACH BAIA DA GUANABARA.
OKAY, NOW I *KNOW* I'M DREAMING.

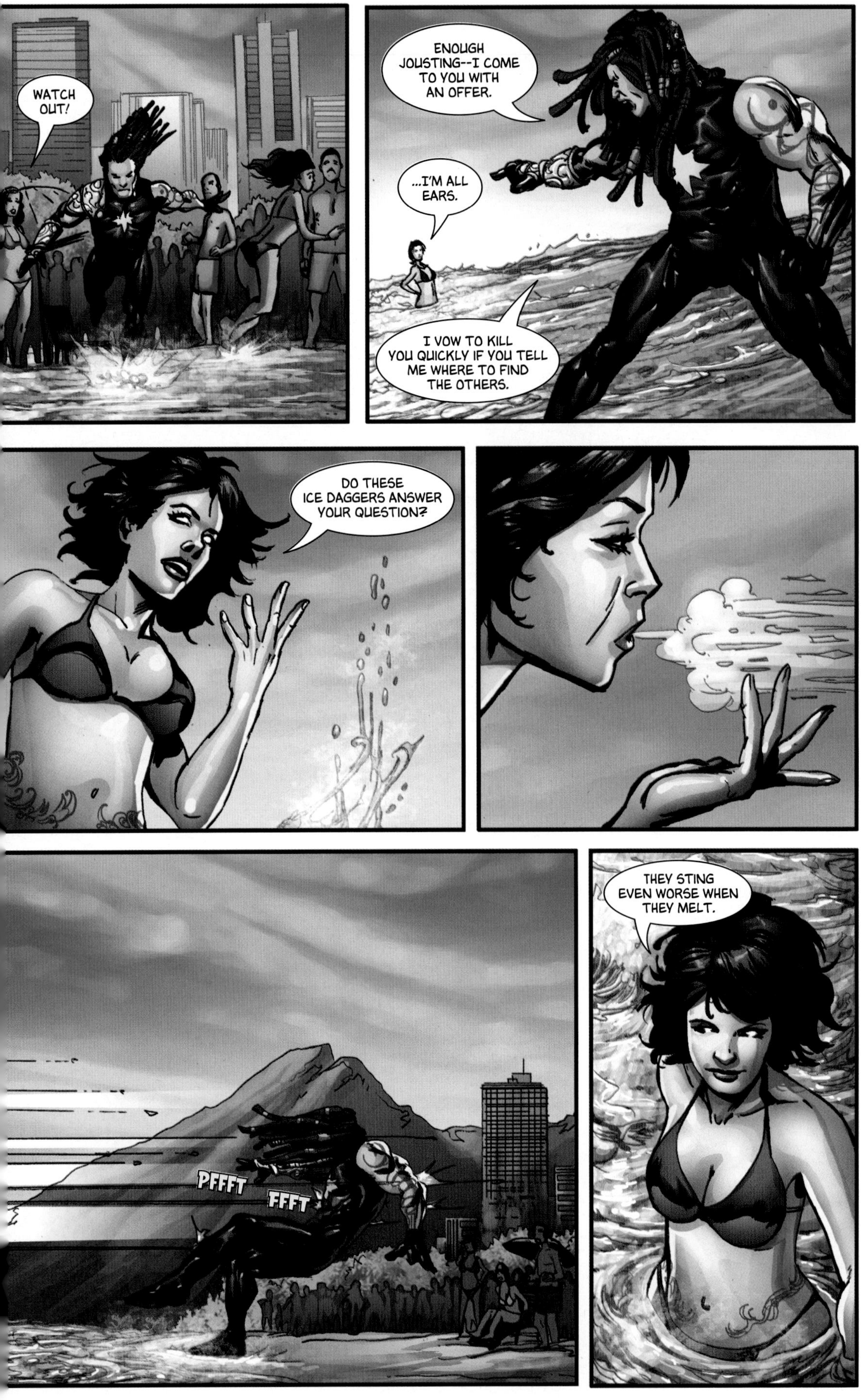
WATCH OUT!
ENOUGH JOUSTING--I COME TO YOU WITH AN OFFER.
...I'M ALL EARS.
I VOW TO KILL YOU QUICKLY IF YOU TELL ME WHERE TO FIND THE OTHERS.
DO THESE ICE DAGGERS ANSWER YOUR QUESTION?
PFFFT
FFFT
THEY STING EVEN WORSE WHEN THEY MELT.

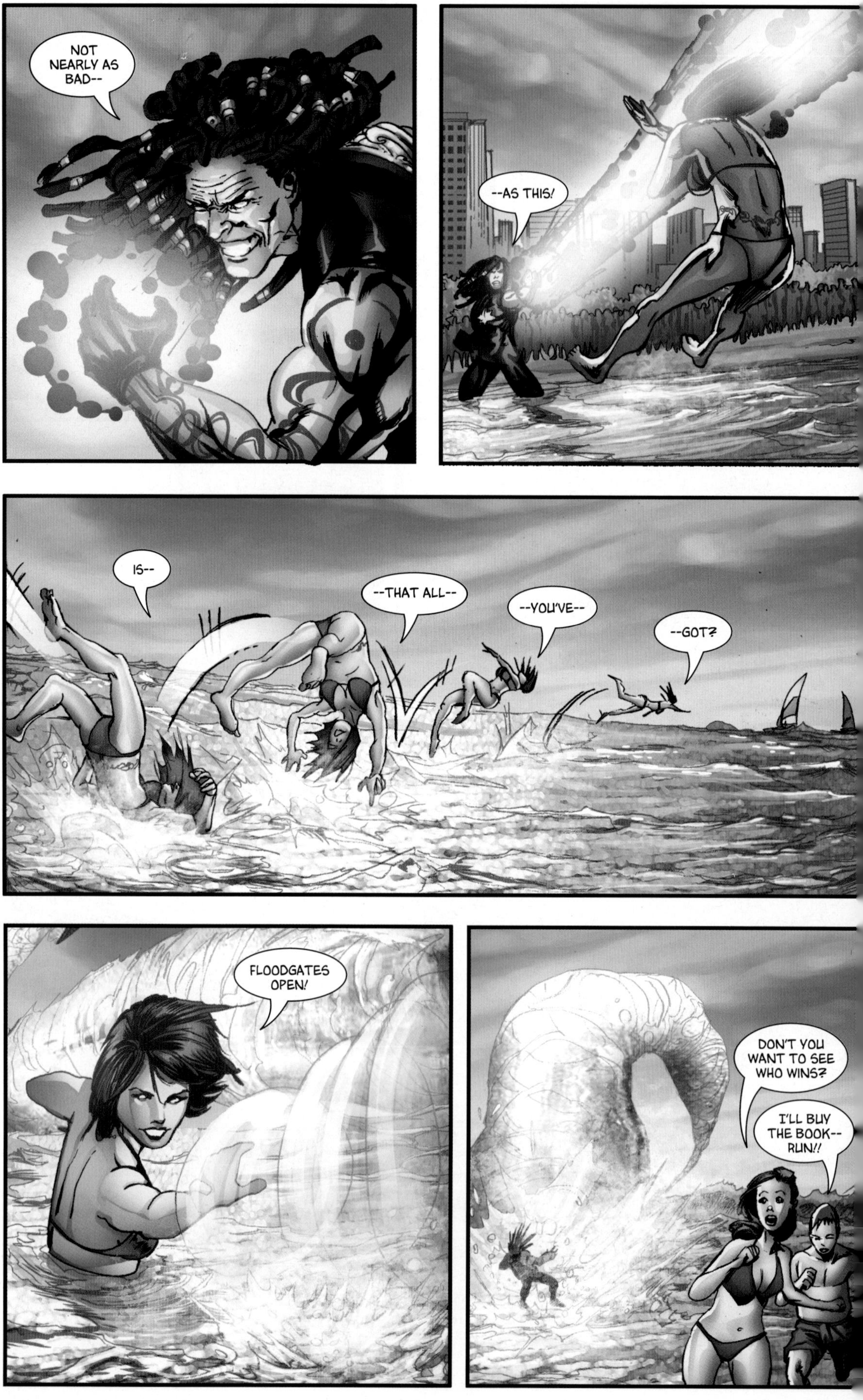
NOT NEARLY AS BAD--
--AS THIS!
IS--
--THAT ALL--
--YOU'VE--
--GOT?
FLOODGATES OPEN!
DON'T YOU WANT TO SEE WHO WINS?
I'LL BUY THE BOOK-- RUN!!

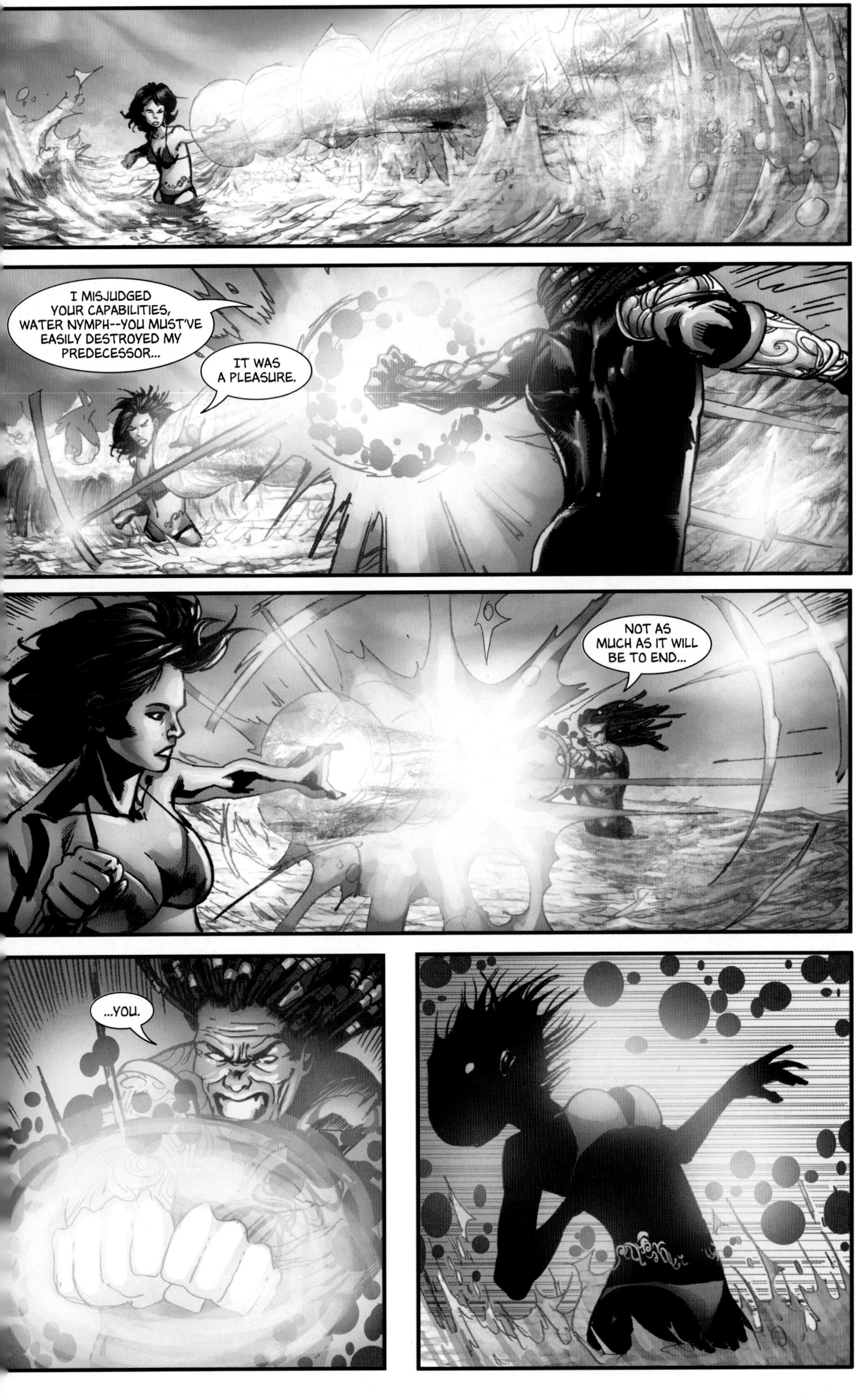
I MISJUDGED YOUR CAPABILITIES, WATER NYMPH--YOU MUST'VE EASILY DESTROYED MY PREDECESSOR...
IT WAS A PLEASURE.
NOT AS MUCH AS IT WILL BE TO END...
...YOU.

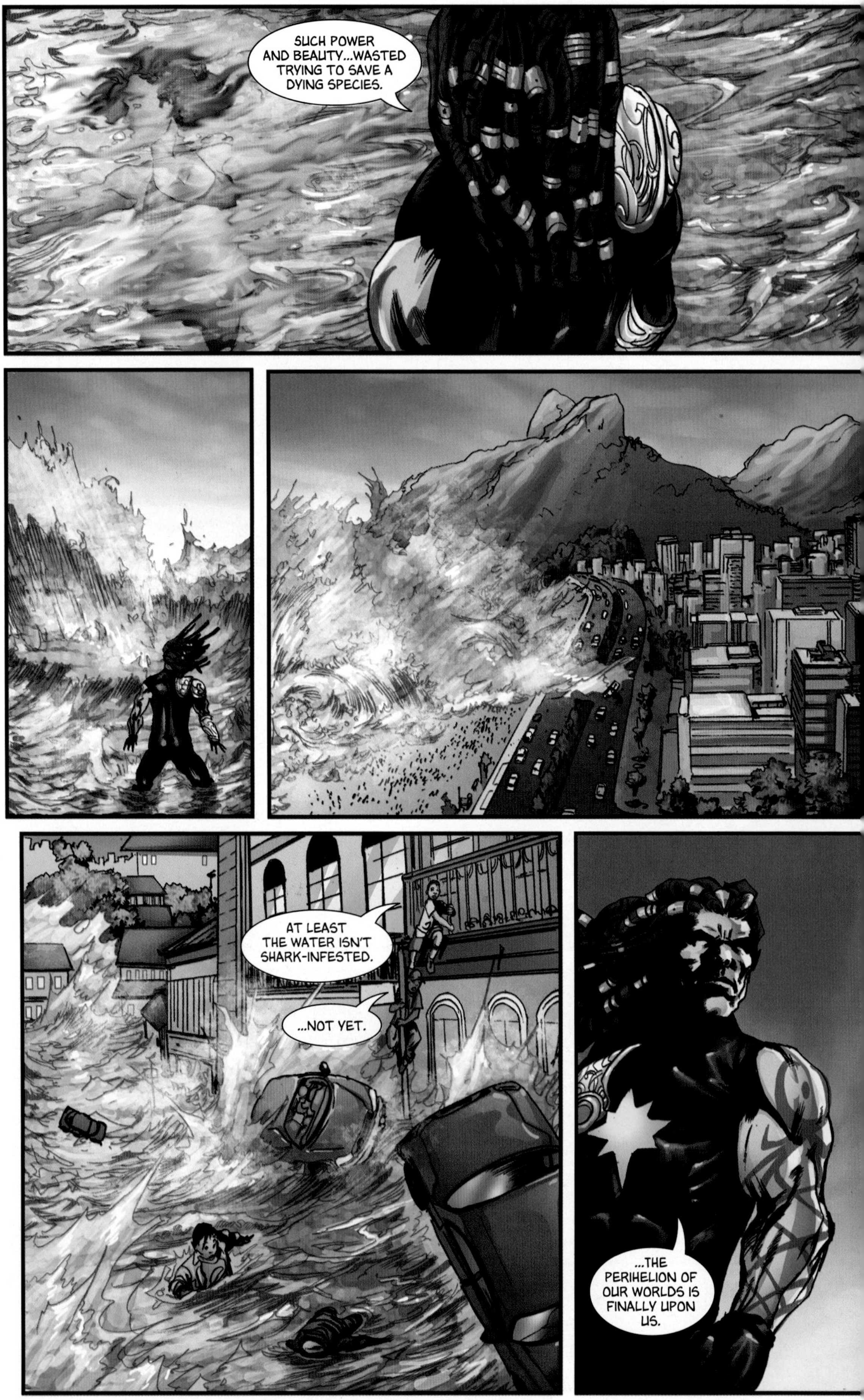
SUCH POWER AND BEAUTY...WASTED TRYING TO SAVE A DYING SPECIES.
AT LEAST THE WATER ISN'T SHARK-INFESTED.
...NOT YET.
...THE PERIHELION OF OUR WORLDS IS FINALLY UPON US.

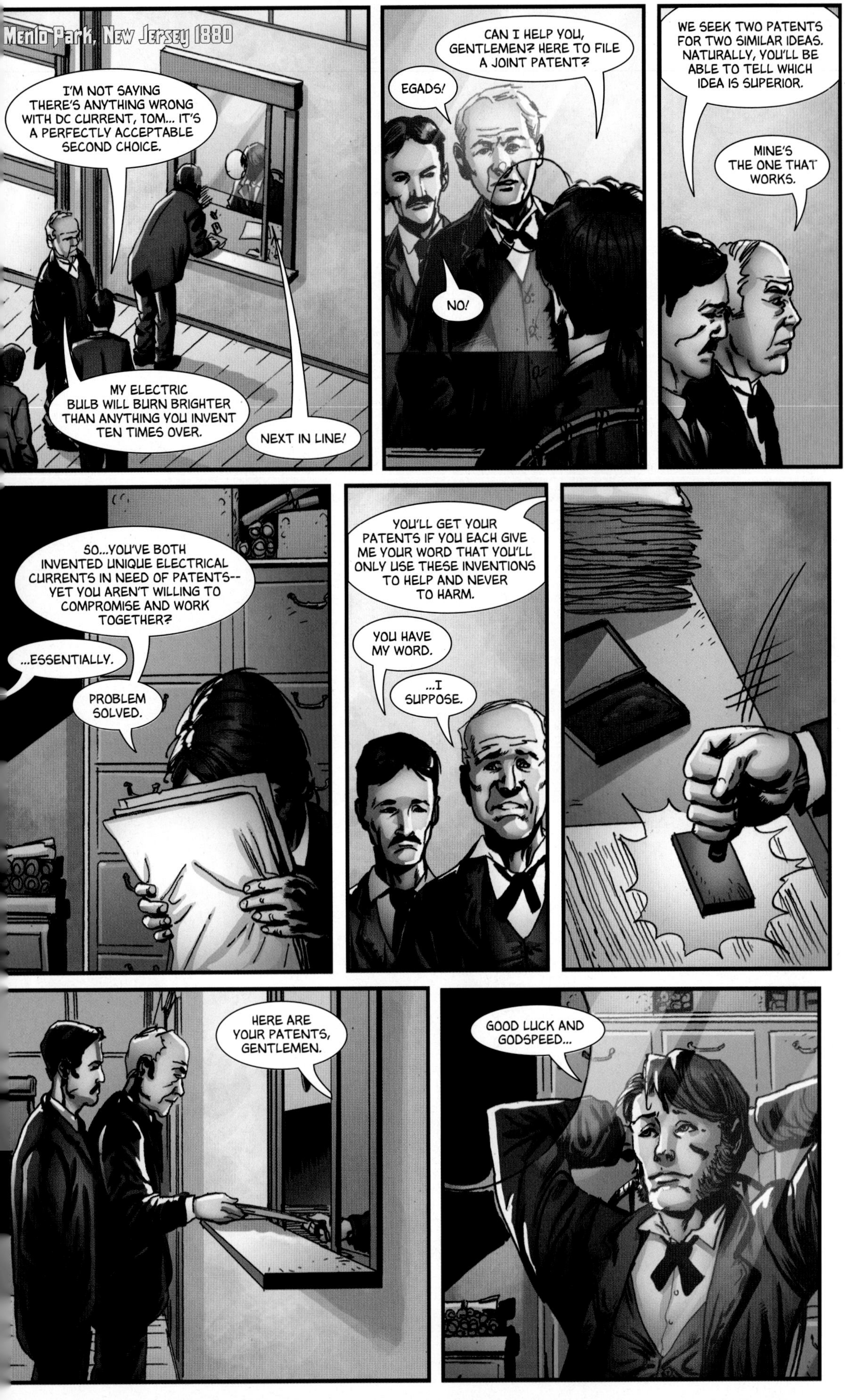
Menlo Park, New Jersey 1880
I'M NOT SAYING THERE'S ANYTHING WRONG WITH DC CURRENT, TOM... IT'S A PERFECTLY ACCEPTABLE SECOND CHOICE.
MY ELECTRIC BULB WILL BURN BRIGHTER THAN ANYTHING YOU INVENT TEN TIMES OVER.
NEXT IN LINE!
CAN I HELP YOU, GENTLEMEN? HERE TO FILE A JOINT PATENT?
EGADS!
NO!
WE SEEK TWO PATENTS FOR TWO SIMILAR IDEAS. NATURALLY, YOU'LL BE ABLE TO TELL WHICH IDEA IS SUPERIOR.
MINE'S THE ONE THAT WORKS.
SO...YOU'VE BOTH INVENTED UNIQUE ELECTRICAL CURRENTS IN NEED OF PATENTS--YET YOU AREN'T WILLING TO COMPROMISE AND WORK TOGETHER?
...ESSENTIALLY.
PROBLEM SOLVED.
YOU'LL GET YOUR PATENTS IF YOU EACH GIVE ME YOUR WORD THAT YOU'LL ONLY USE THESE INVENTIONS TO HELP AND NEVER TO HARM.
YOU HAVE MY WORD.
...I SUPPOSE.
HERE ARE YOUR PATENTS, GENTLEMEN.
GOOD LUCK AND GODSPEED...

San Juan Islands

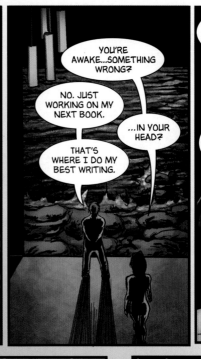

YOU'RE AWAKE...SOMETHING WRONG?

NO. JUST WORKING ON MY NEXT BOOK.

...IN YOUR HEAD?

THAT'S WHERE I DO MY BEST WRITING.

I KNOW YOU HATE IT WHEN I ASK, BUT DO WE HAVE ANY PLANS FOR DINNER TONIGHT?

NO. SHOULD WE? WAIT--WHAT'S TONIGHT?

IF YOU AREN'T IN A TUX WHEN I GET OUT OF THE SHOWER, YOU'RE DEAD TO ME.

HAPPY TWO-YEAR ANNIVERSARY.

YOU REMEMBERED.

HOW COULD I FORGET.

I JUST KNOW HOW YOU GET ABOUT BIRTHDAYS AND ANNIVERSARIES... THIS REALLY MEANS A LOT TO ME.

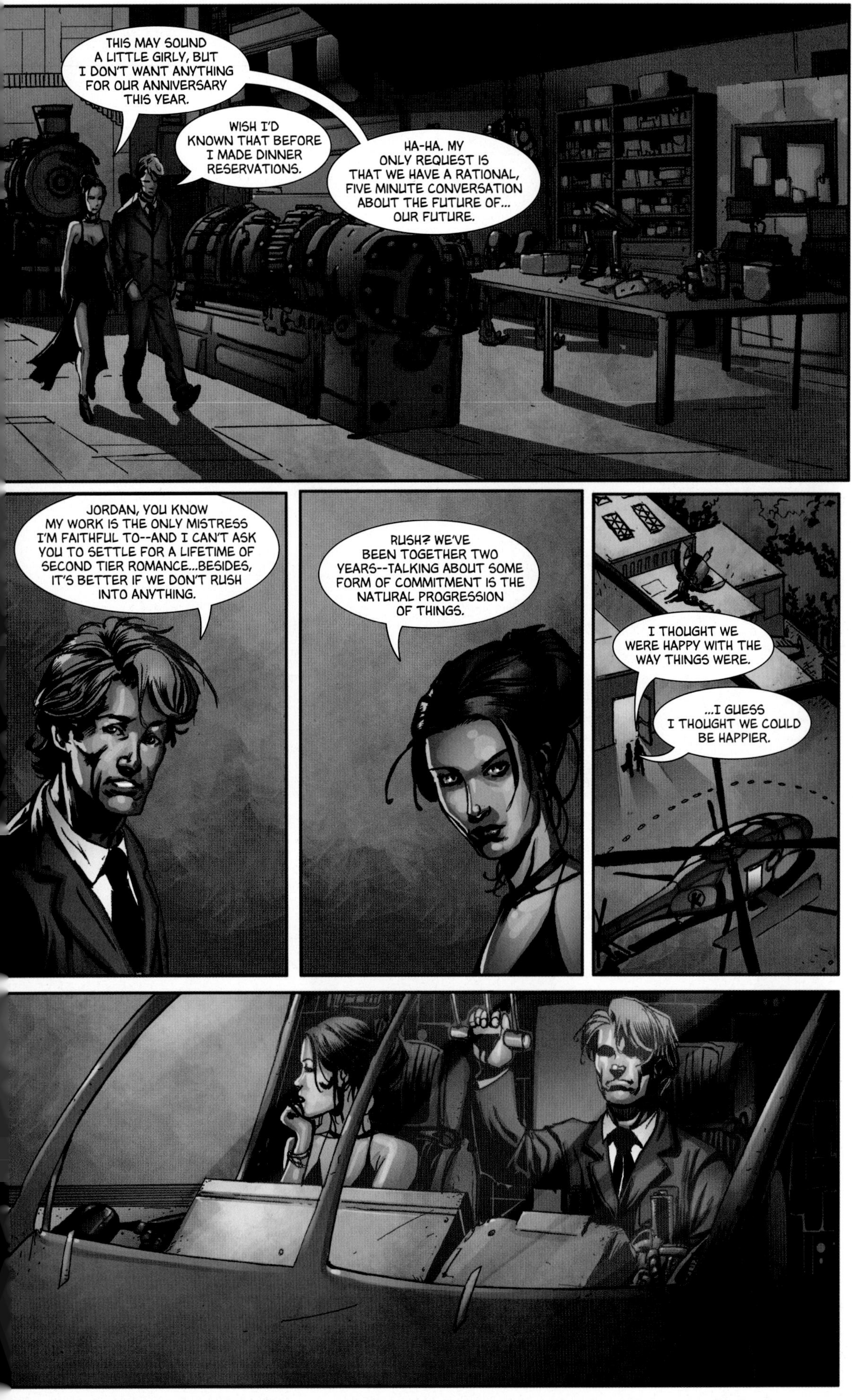
THIS MAY SOUND A LITTLE GIRLY, BUT I DON'T WANT ANYTHING FOR OUR ANNIVERSARY THIS YEAR.
WISH I'D KNOWN THAT BEFORE I MADE DINNER RESERVATIONS.
HA-HA. MY ONLY REQUEST IS THAT WE HAVE A RATIONAL, FIVE MINUTE CONVERSATION ABOUT THE FUTURE OF... OUR FUTURE.
JORDAN, YOU KNOW MY WORK IS THE ONLY MISTRESS I'M FAITHFUL TO--AND I CAN'T ASK YOU TO SETTLE FOR A LIFETIME OF SECOND TIER ROMANCE...BESIDES, IT'S BETTER IF WE DON'T RUSH INTO ANYTHING.
RUSH? WE'VE BEEN TOGETHER TWO YEARS--TALKING ABOUT SOME FORM OF COMMITMENT IS THE NATURAL PROGRESSION OF THINGS.
I THOUGHT WE WERE HAPPY WITH THE WAY THINGS WERE.
...I GUESS I THOUGHT WE COULD BE HAPPIER.

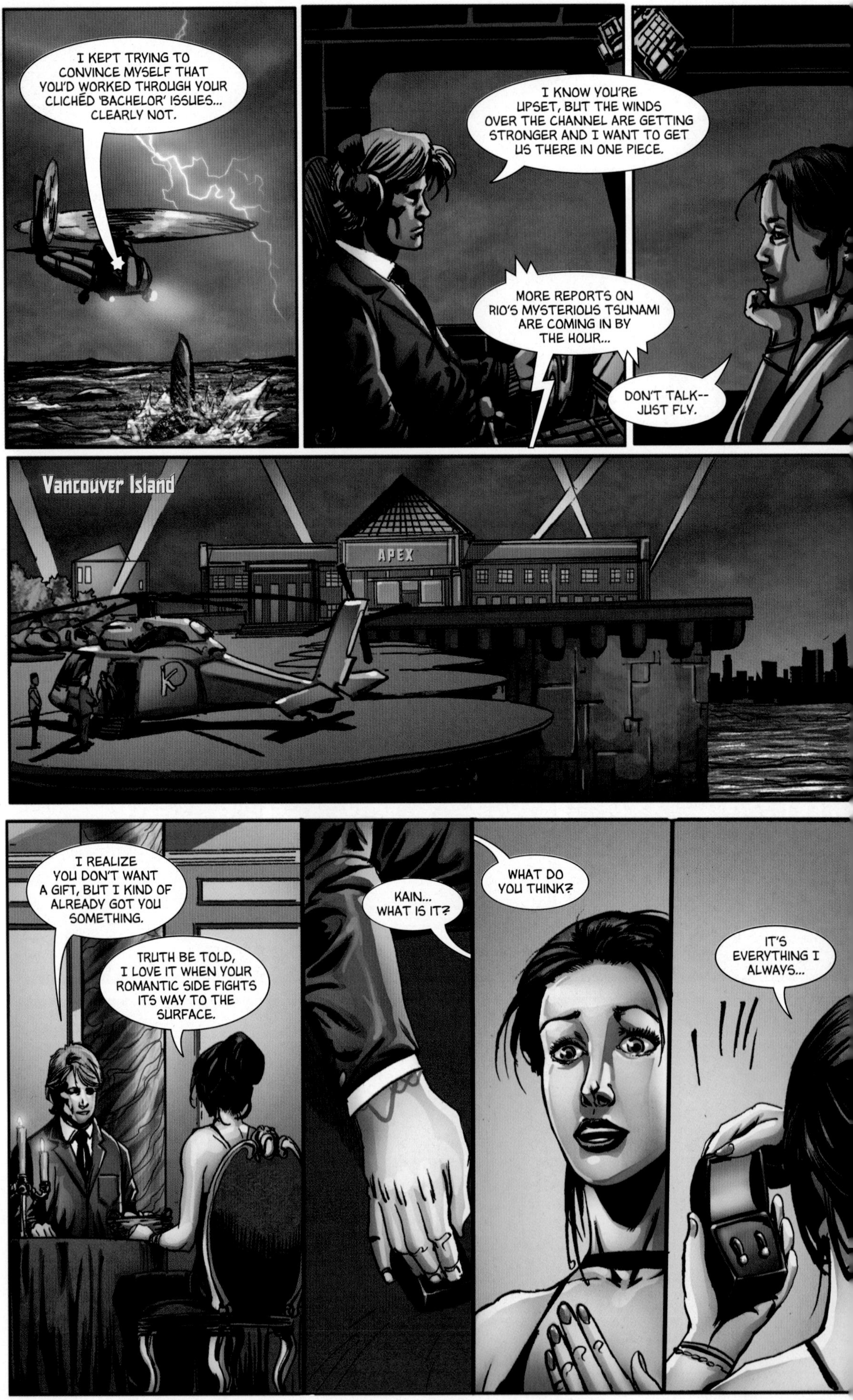
I KEPT TRYING TO CONVINCE MYSELF THAT YOU'D WORKED THROUGH YOUR CLICHÉD 'BACHELOR' ISSUES... CLEARLY NOT.
I KNOW YOU'RE UPSET, BUT THE WINDS OVER THE CHANNEL ARE GETTING STRONGER AND I WANT TO GET US THERE IN ONE PIECE.
MORE REPORTS ON RIO'S MYSTERIOUS TSUNAMI ARE COMING IN BY THE HOUR...
DON'T TALK-- JUST FLY.
Vancouver Island
APEX
I REALIZE YOU DON'T WANT A GIFT, BUT I KIND OF ALREADY GOT YOU SOMETHING.
TRUTH BE TOLD, I LOVE IT WHEN YOUR ROMANTIC SIDE FIGHTS ITS WAY TO THE SURFACE.
KAIN... WHAT IS IT?
WHAT DO YOU THINK?
IT'S EVERYTHING I ALWAYS...

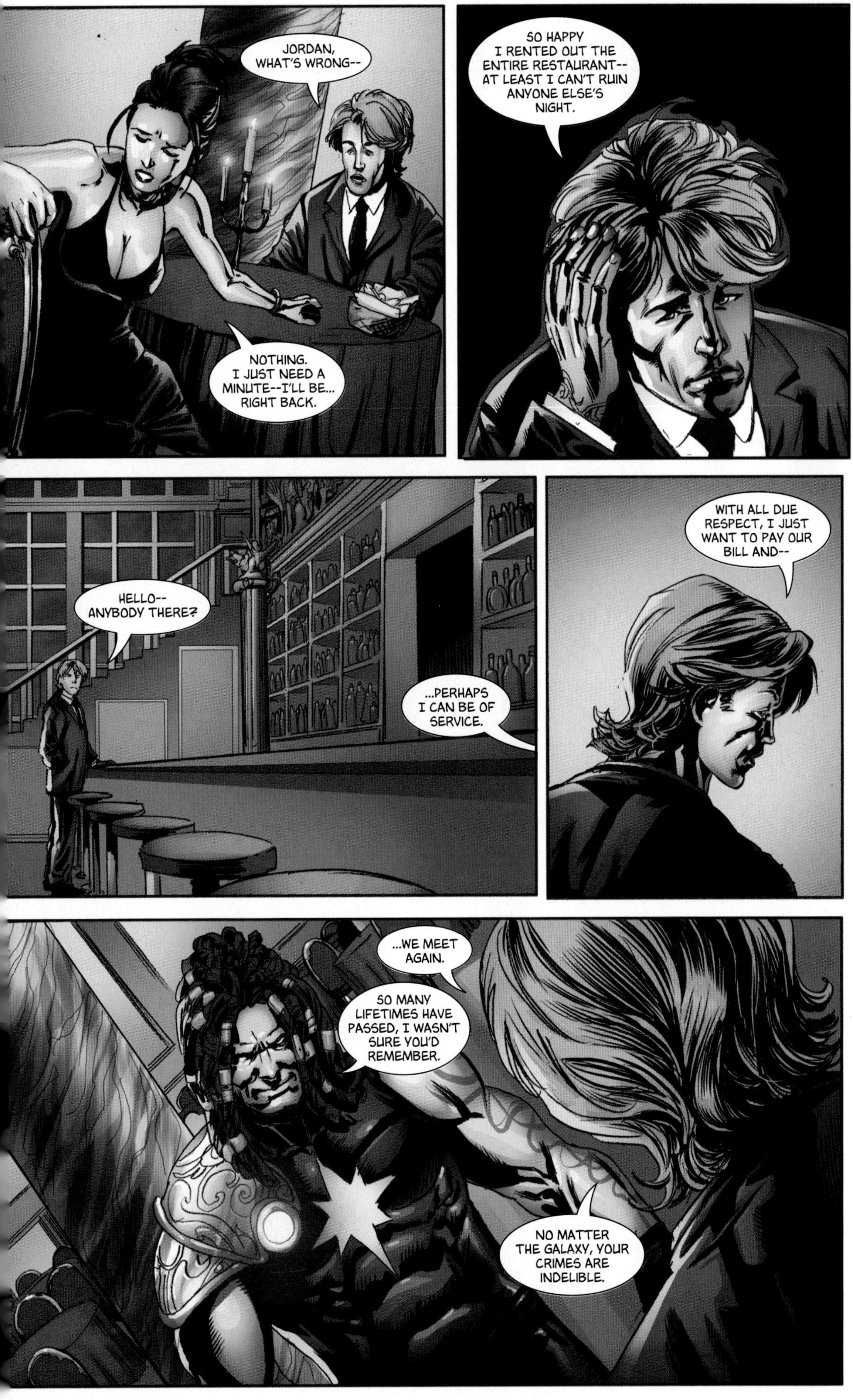
JORDAN, WHAT'S WRONG--
NOTHING. I JUST NEED A MINUTE--I'LL BE... RIGHT BACK.
SO HAPPY I RENTED OUT THE ENTIRE RESTAURANT-- AT LEAST I CAN'T RUIN ANYONE ELSE'S NIGHT.
HELLO-- ANYBODY THERE?
...PERHAPS I CAN BE OF SERVICE.
WITH ALL DUE RESPECT, I JUST WANT TO PAY OUR BILL AND--
...WE MEET AGAIN.
SO MANY LIFETIMES HAVE PASSED, I WASN'T SURE YOU'D REMEMBER.
NO MATTER THE GALAXY, YOUR CRIMES ARE INDELIBLE.

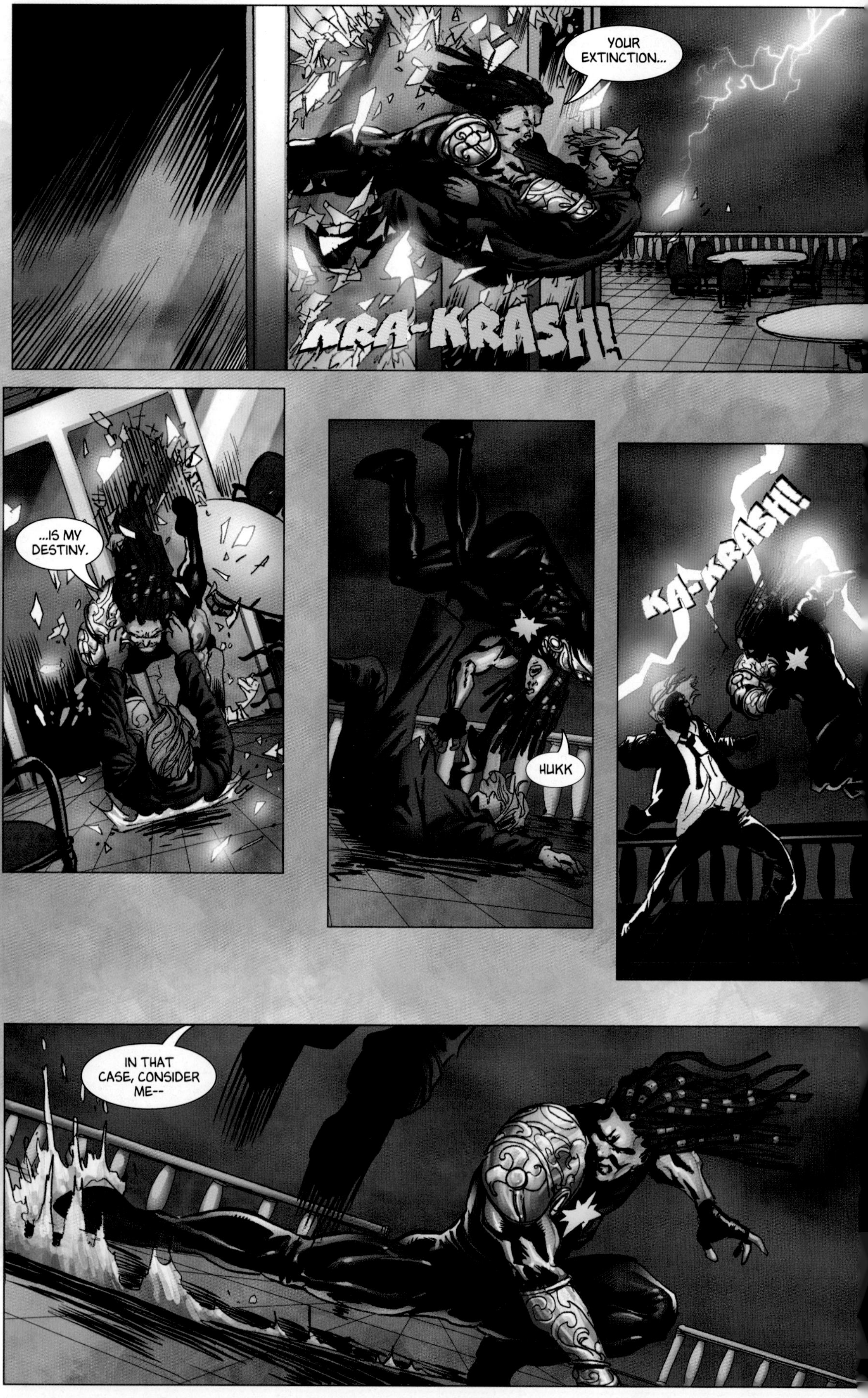
YOUR EXTINCTION...
KRA-KRASH!
...IS MY DESTINY.
HUKK
KA-KRASH!!
IN THAT CASE, CONSIDER ME--

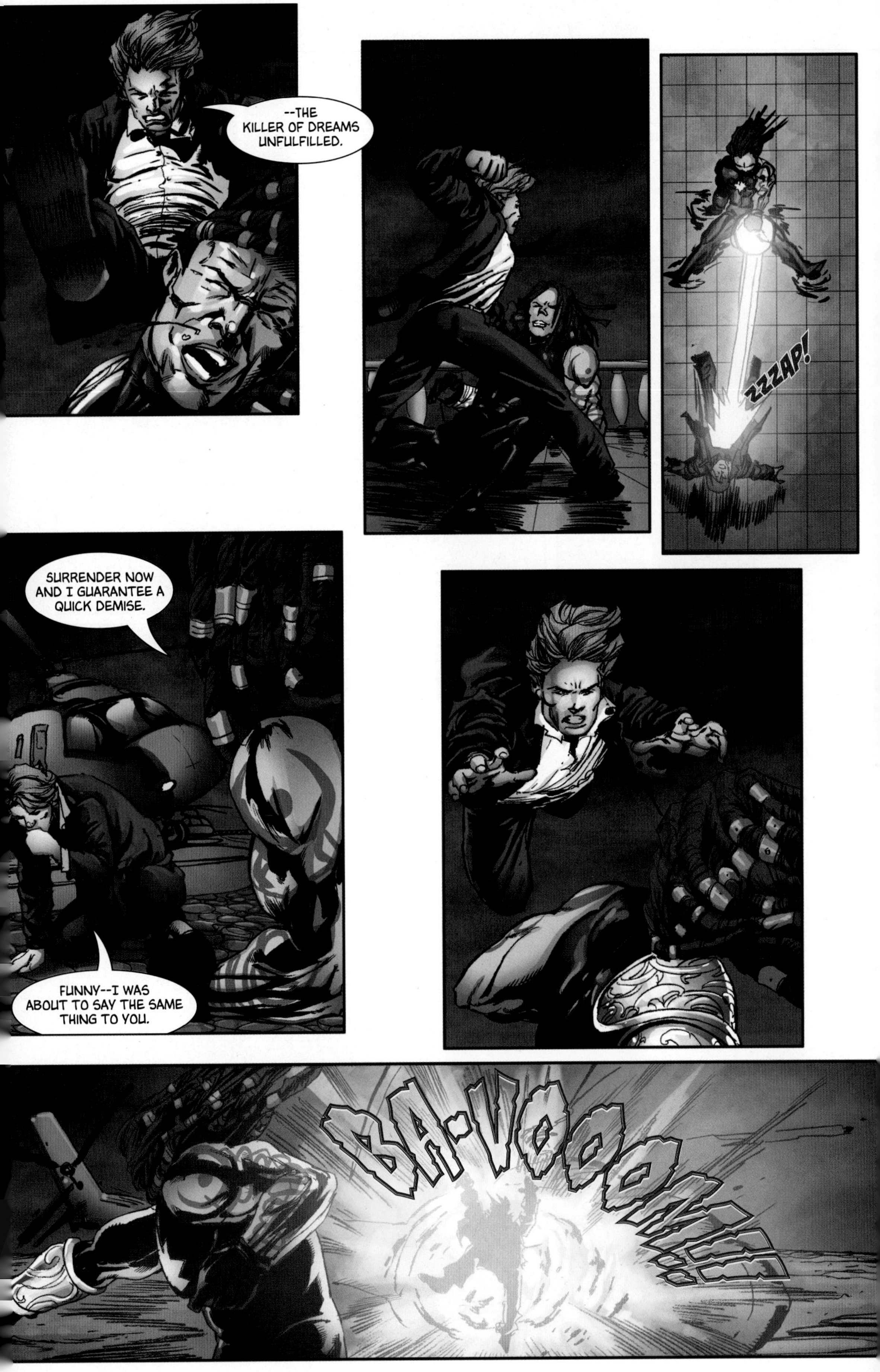
--THE KILLER OF DREAMS UNFULFILLED.
ZZZAP!
SURRENDER NOW AND I GUARANTEE A QUICK DEMISE.
FUNNY--I WAS ABOUT TO SAY THE SAME THING TO YOU.
BA-VOOOOM!!

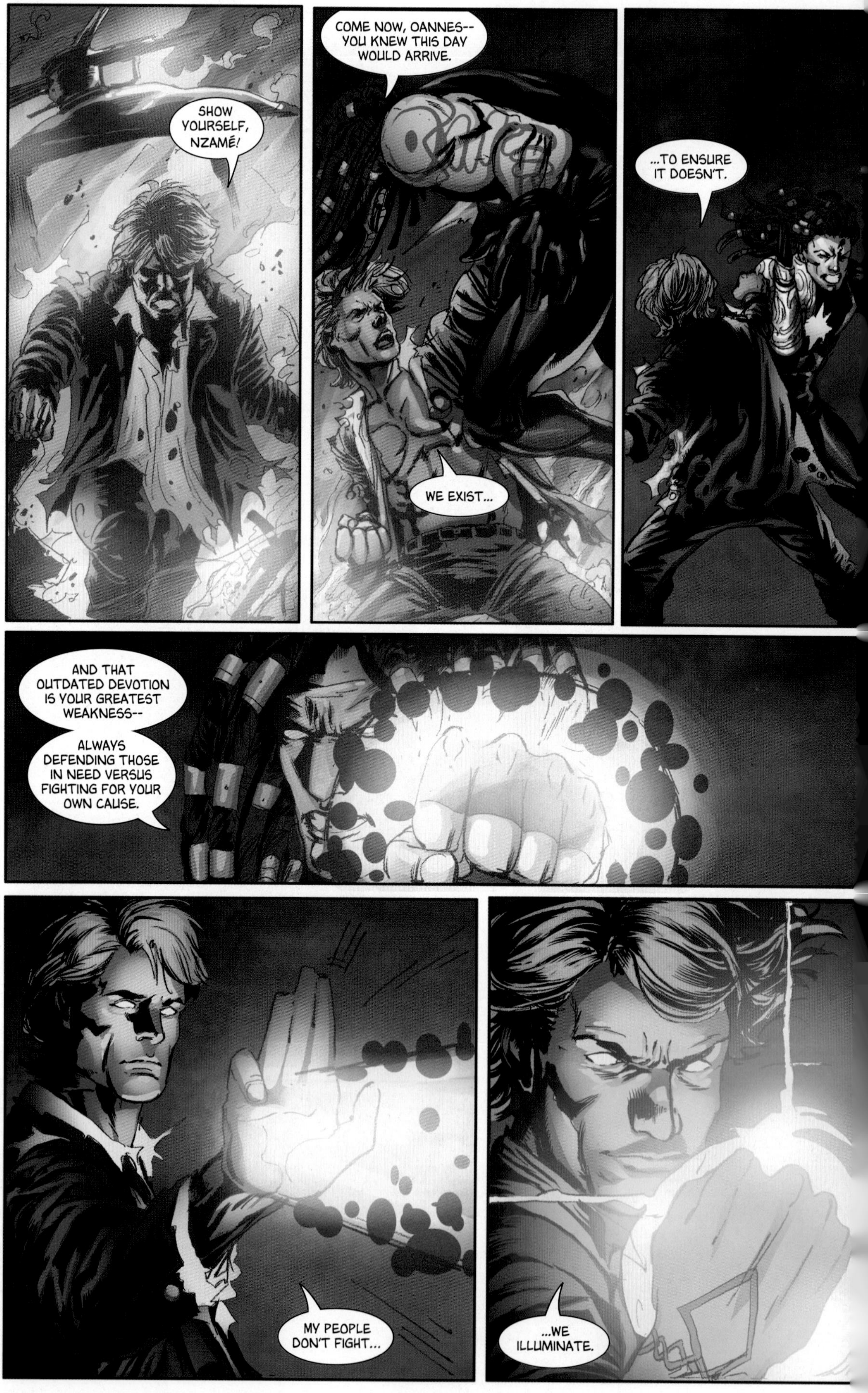
SHOW YOURSELF, NZAMÉ!
COME NOW, OANNES-- YOU KNEW THIS DAY WOULD ARRIVE.
WE EXIST...
...TO ENSURE IT DOESN'T.
AND THAT OUTDATED DEVOTION IS YOUR GREATEST WEAKNESS--
ALWAYS DEFENDING THOSE IN NEED VERSUS FIGHTING FOR YOUR OWN CAUSE.
MY PEOPLE DON'T FIGHT...
...WE ILLUMINATE.

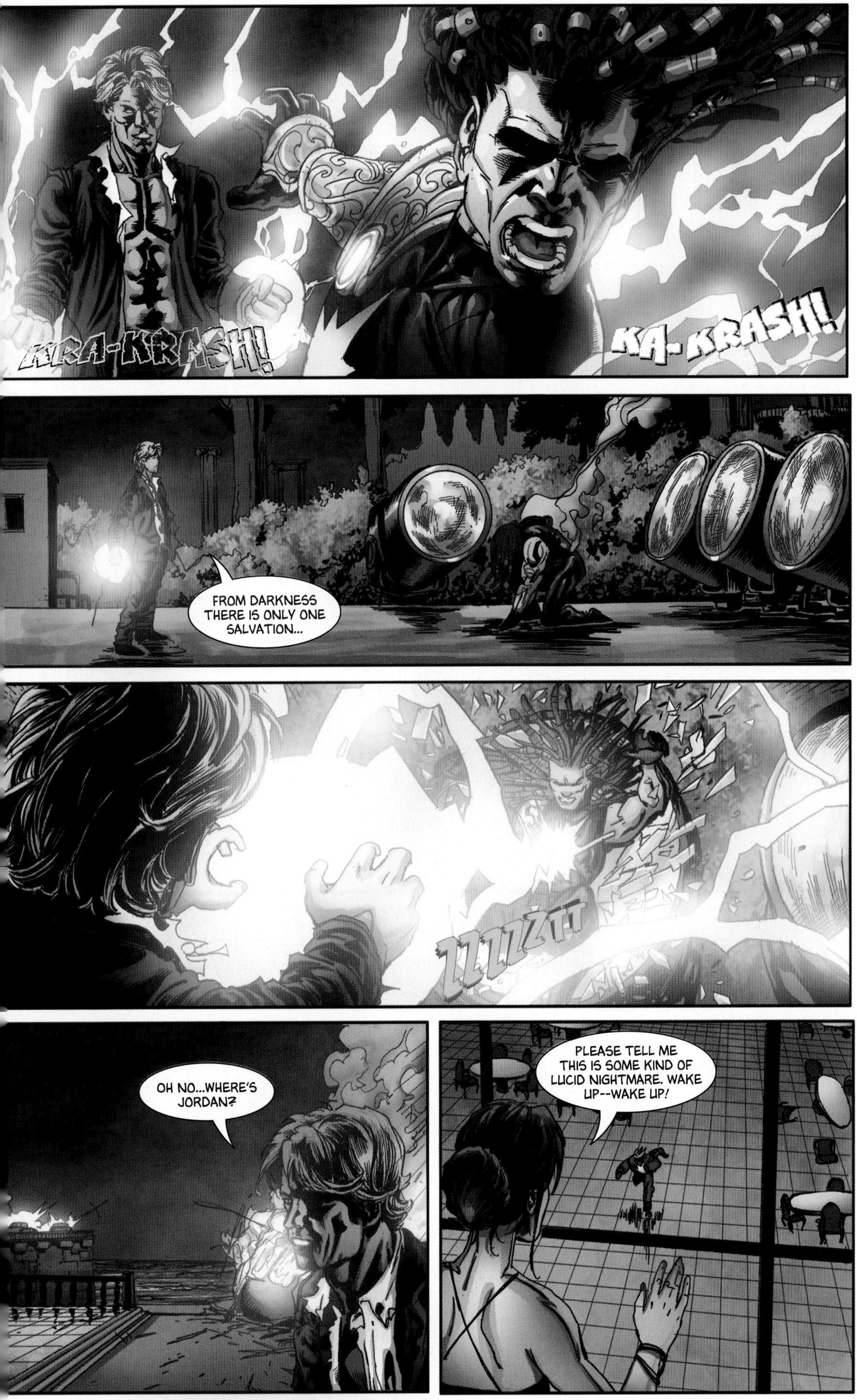
KRA-KRASH!
KA-KRASH!
FROM DARKNESS THERE IS ONLY ONE SALVATION...
ZZZZZTT
OH NO...WHERE'S JORDAN?
PLEASE TELL ME THIS IS SOME KIND OF LUCID NIGHTMARE. WAKE UP--WAKE UP!

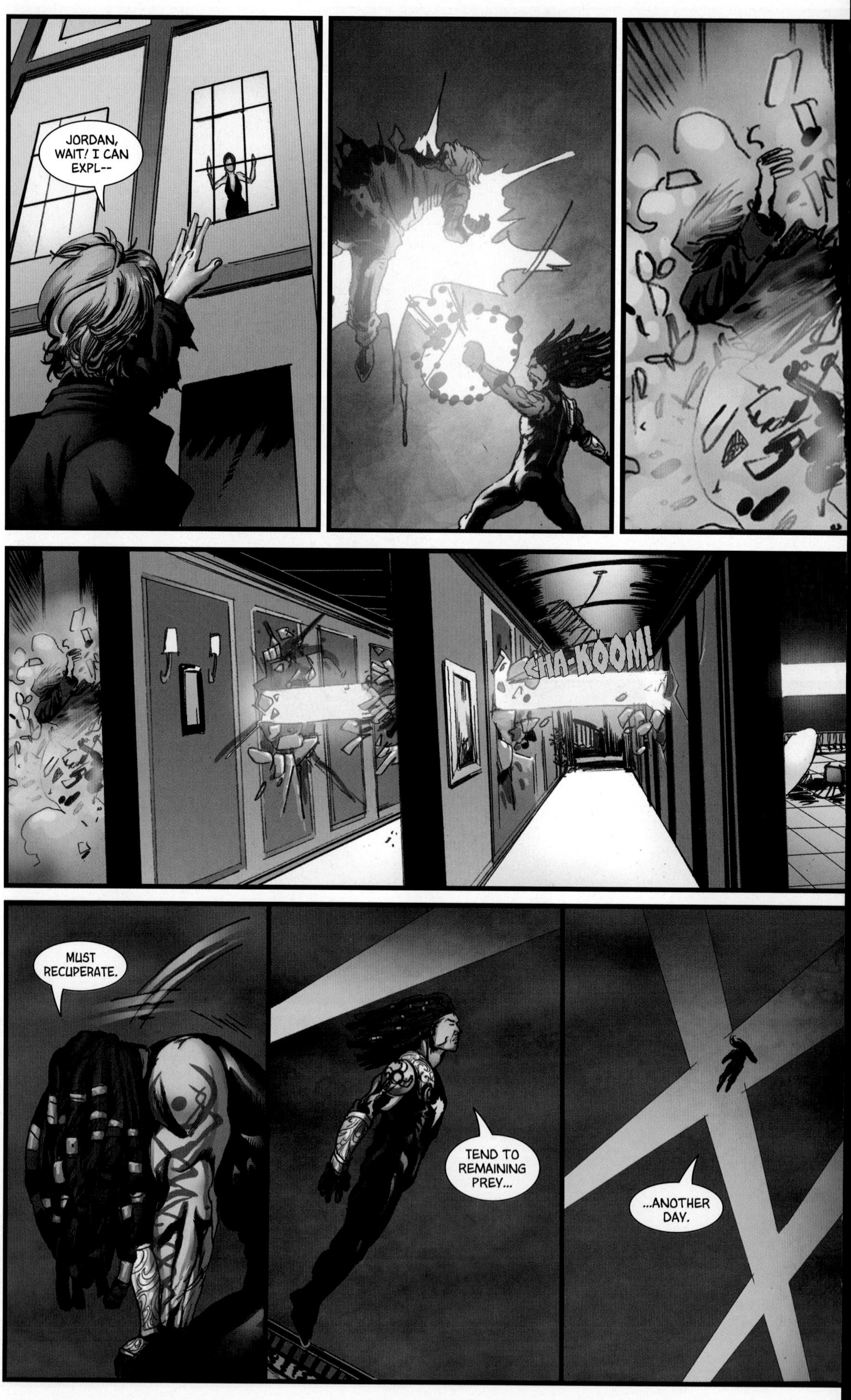
JORDAN, WAIT! I CAN EXPL--
CHA-KOOM!
MUST RECUPERATE.
TEND TO REMAINING PREY...
...ANOTHER DAY.

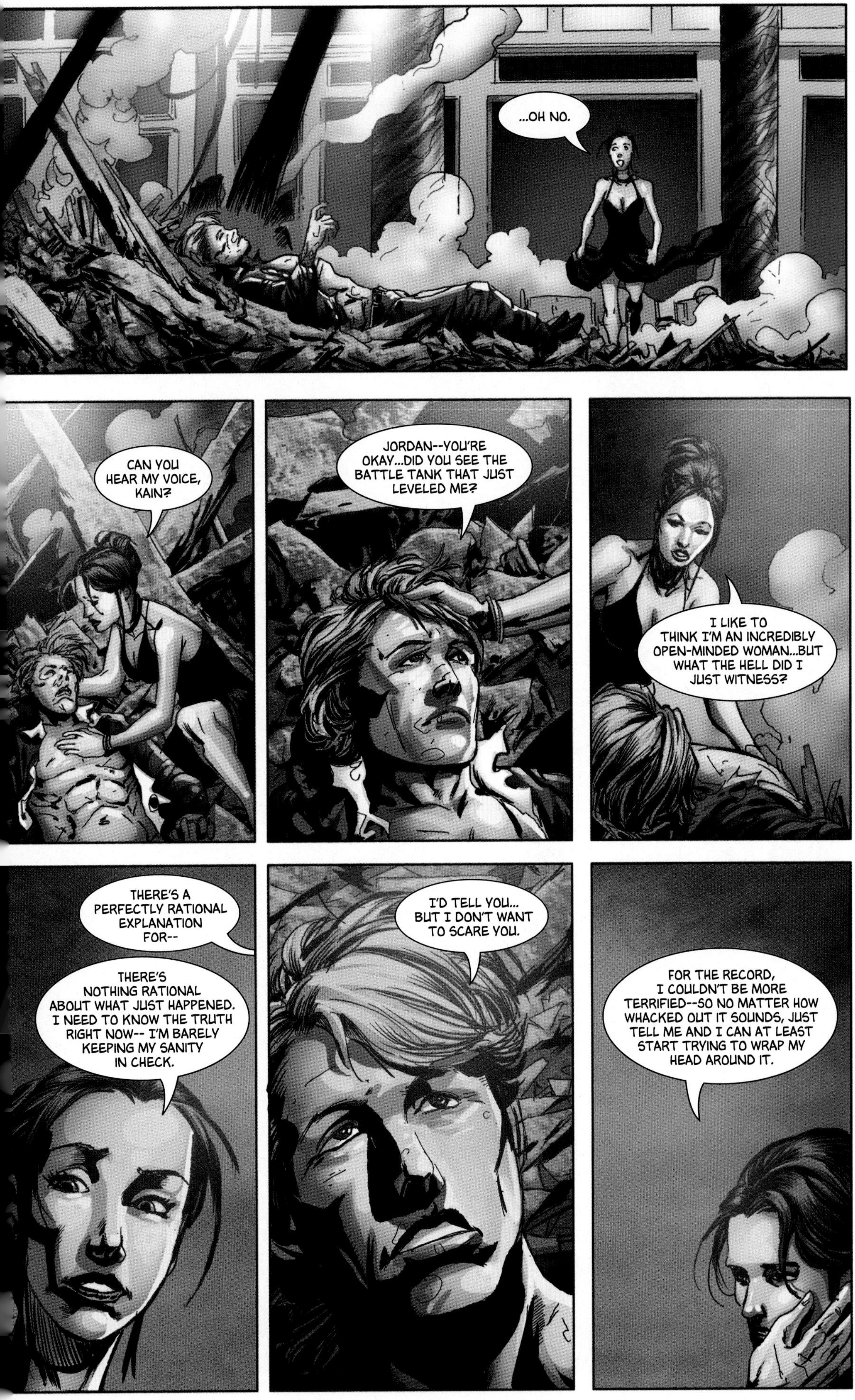
...OH NO.
CAN YOU HEAR MY VOICE, KAIN?
JORDAN--YOU'RE OKAY...DID YOU SEE THE BATTLE TANK THAT JUST LEVELED ME?
I LIKE TO THINK I'M AN INCREDIBLY OPEN-MINDED WOMAN...BUT WHAT THE HELL DID I JUST WITNESS?
THERE'S A PERFECTLY RATIONAL EXPLANATION FOR--
THERE'S NOTHING RATIONAL ABOUT WHAT JUST HAPPENED. I NEED TO KNOW THE TRUTH RIGHT NOW-- I'M BARELY KEEPING MY SANITY IN CHECK.
I'D TELL YOU... BUT I DON'T WANT TO SCARE YOU.
FOR THE RECORD, I COULDN'T BE MORE TERRIFIED--SO NO MATTER HOW WHACKED OUT IT SOUNDS, JUST TELL ME AND I CAN AT LEAST START TRYING TO WRAP MY HEAD AROUND IT.

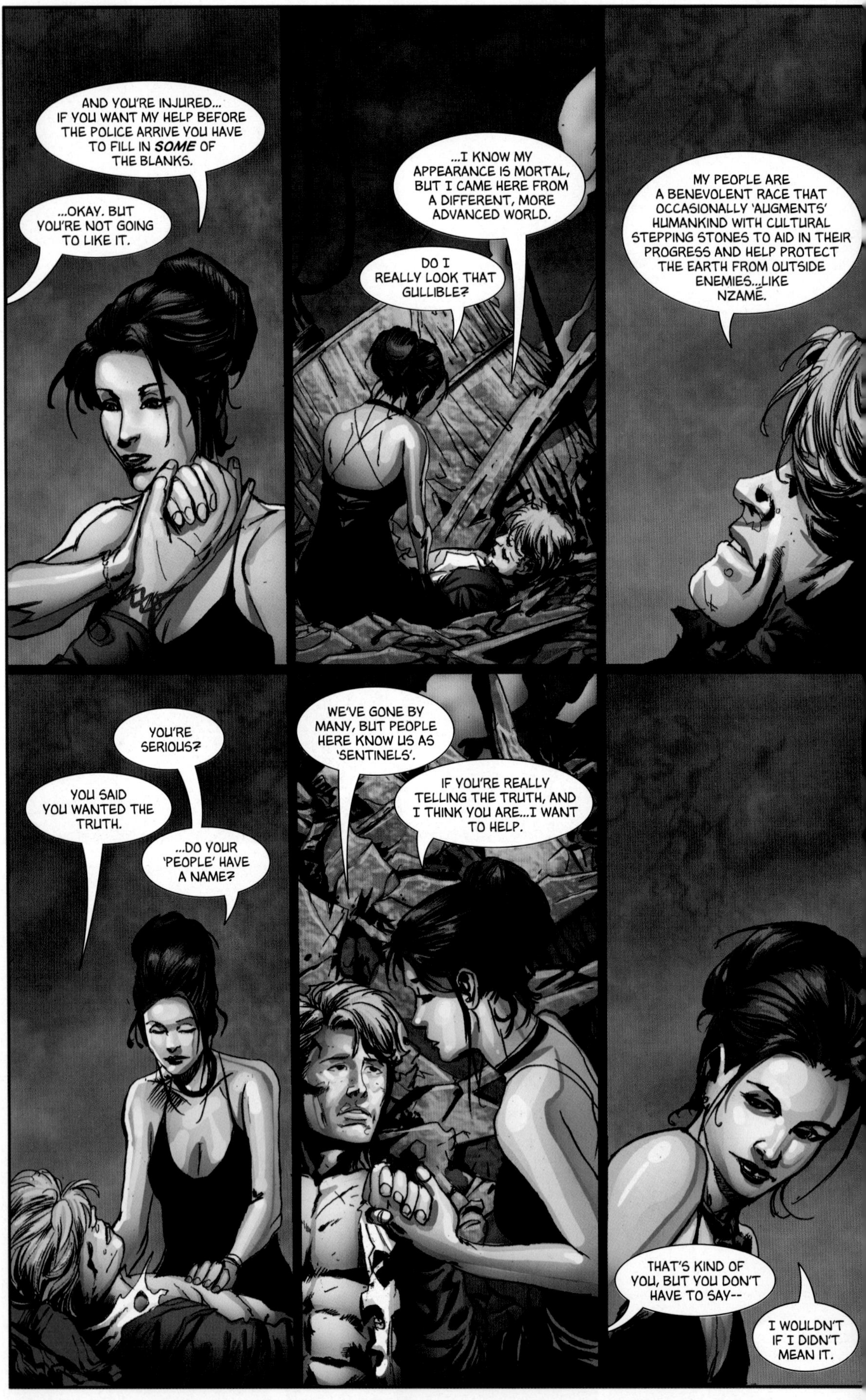
AND YOU'RE INJURED... IF YOU WANT MY HELP BEFORE THE POLICE ARRIVE YOU HAVE TO FILL IN *SOME* OF THE BLANKS.
...OKAY. BUT YOU'RE NOT GOING TO LIKE IT.
...I KNOW MY APPEARANCE IS MORTAL, BUT I CAME HERE FROM A DIFFERENT, MORE ADVANCED WORLD.
DO I REALLY LOOK THAT GULLIBLE?
MY PEOPLE ARE A BENEVOLENT RACE THAT OCCASIONALLY 'AUGMENTS' HUMANKIND WITH CULTURAL STEPPING STONES TO AID IN THEIR PROGRESS AND HELP PROTECT THE EARTH FROM OUTSIDE ENEMIES...LIKE NZAMÉ.
YOU'RE SERIOUS?
YOU SAID YOU WANTED THE TRUTH.
...DO YOUR 'PEOPLE' HAVE A NAME?
WE'VE GONE BY MANY, BUT PEOPLE HERE KNOW US AS 'SENTINELS'.
IF YOU'RE REALLY TELLING THE TRUTH, AND I THINK YOU ARE...I WANT TO HELP.
THAT'S KIND OF YOU, BUT YOU DON'T HAVE TO SAY--
I WOULDN'T IF I DIDN'T MEAN IT.

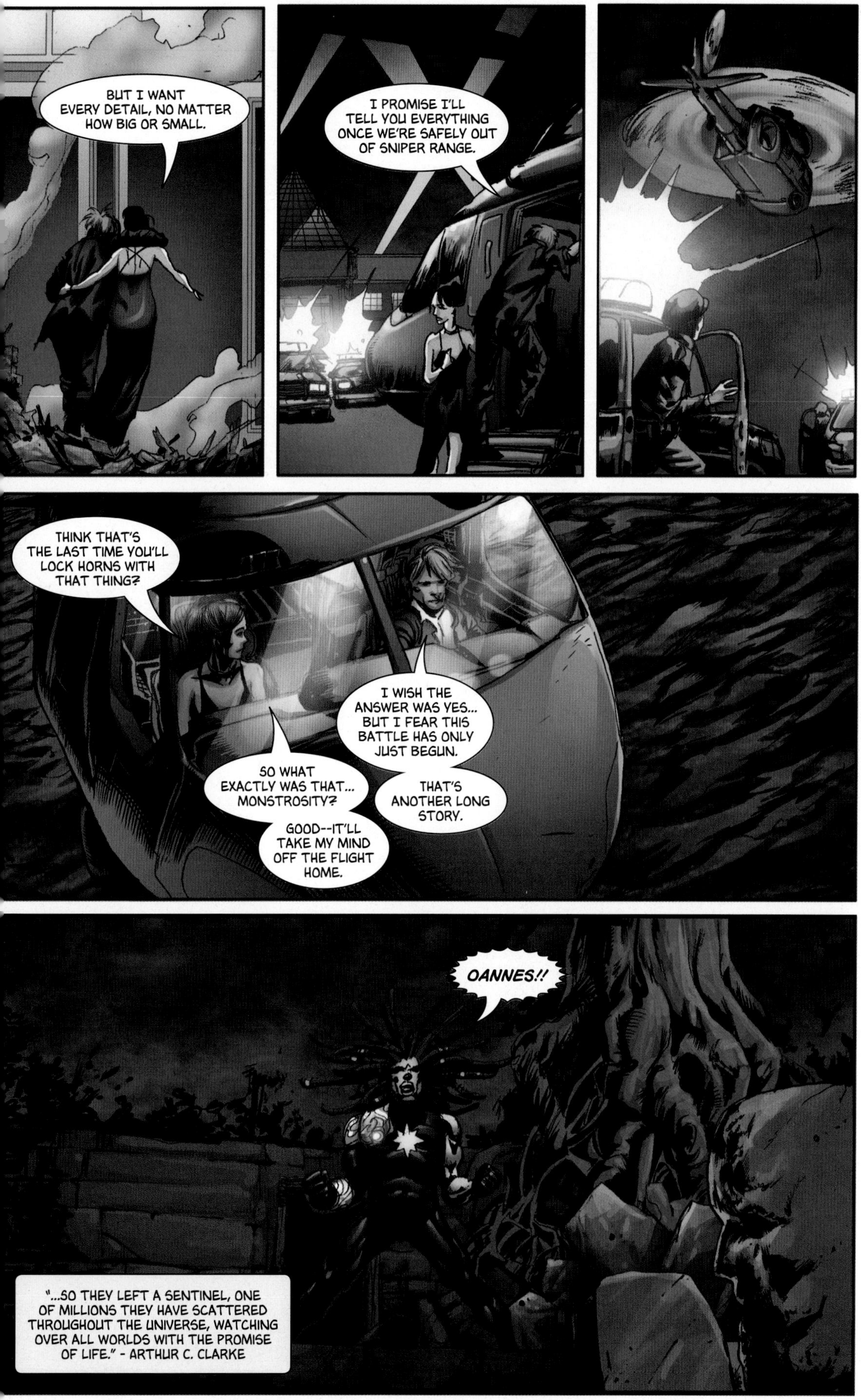

BUT I WANT EVERY DETAIL, NO MATTER HOW BIG OR SMALL.
I PROMISE I'LL TELL YOU EVERYTHING ONCE WE'RE SAFELY OUT OF SNIPER RANGE.
THINK THAT'S THE LAST TIME YOU'LL LOCK HORNS WITH THAT THING?
I WISH THE ANSWER WAS YES... BUT I FEAR THIS BATTLE HAS ONLY JUST BEGUN.
SO WHAT EXACTLY WAS THAT... MONSTROSITY?
THAT'S ANOTHER LONG STORY.
GOOD--IT'LL TAKE MY MIND OFF THE FLIGHT HOME.
OANNES!!
"...SO THEY LEFT A SENTINEL, ONE OF MILLIONS THEY HAVE SCATTERED THROUGHOUT THE UNIVERSE, WATCHING OVER ALL WORLDS WITH THE PROMISE OF LIFE." - ARTHUR C. CLARKE

# PART TWO

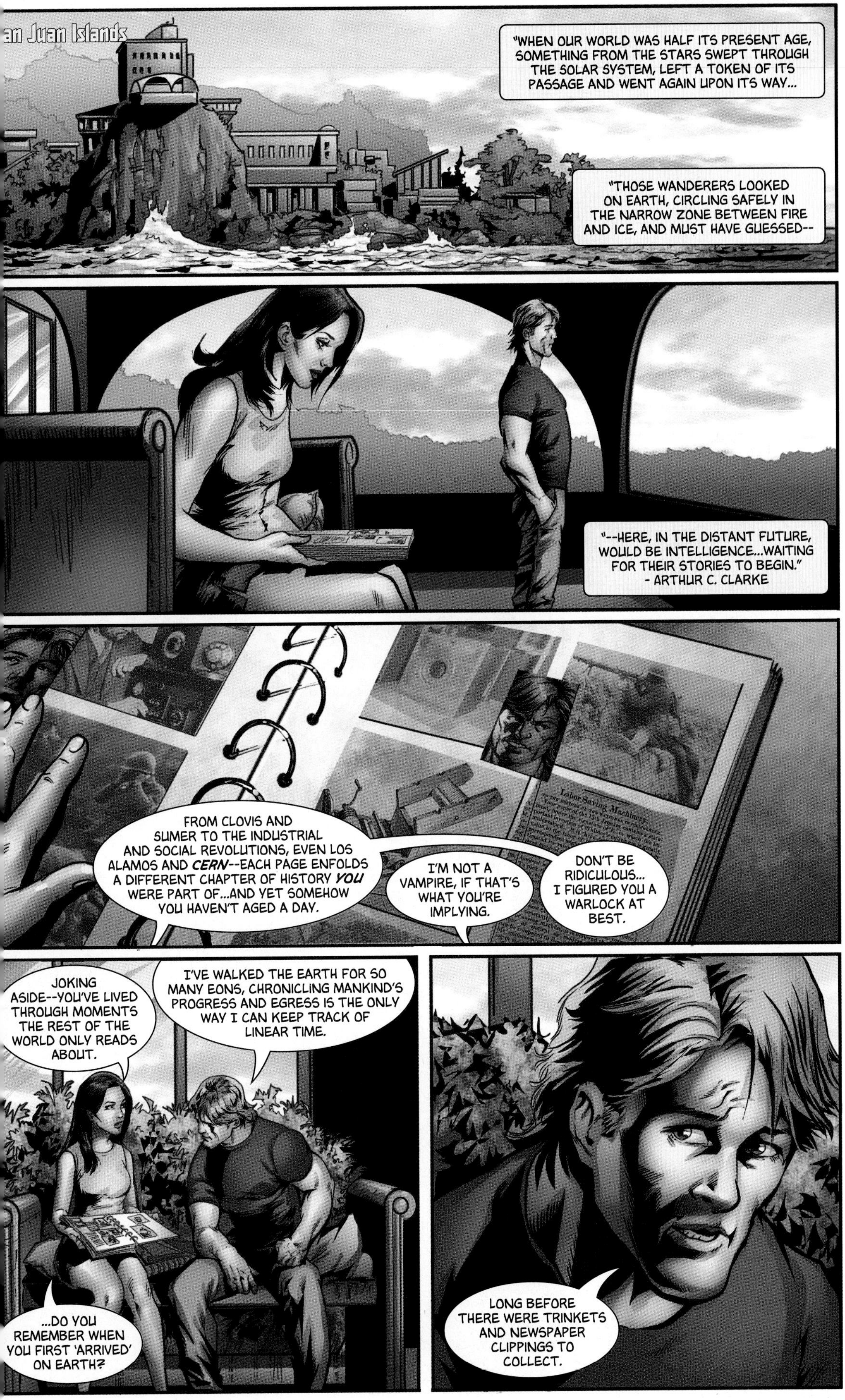
an Juan Islands
"WHEN OUR WORLD WAS HALF ITS PRESENT AGE, SOMETHING FROM THE STARS SWEPT THROUGH THE SOLAR SYSTEM, LEFT A TOKEN OF ITS PASSAGE AND WENT AGAIN UPON ITS WAY...
"THOSE WANDERERS LOOKED ON EARTH, CIRCLING SAFELY IN THE NARROW ZONE BETWEEN FIRE AND ICE, AND MUST HAVE GUESSED--
"--HERE, IN THE DISTANT FUTURE, WOULD BE INTELLIGENCE...WAITING FOR THEIR STORIES TO BEGIN." - ARTHUR C. CLARKE
Labor Saving Machinery.
FROM CLOVIS AND SUMER TO THE INDUSTRIAL AND SOCIAL REVOLUTIONS, EVEN LOS ALAMOS AND *CERN*--EACH PAGE ENFOLDS A DIFFERENT CHAPTER OF HISTORY *YOU* WERE PART OF...AND YET SOMEHOW YOU HAVEN'T AGED A DAY.
I'M NOT A VAMPIRE, IF THAT'S WHAT YOU'RE IMPLYING.
DON'T BE RIDICULOUS... I FIGURED YOU A WARLOCK AT BEST.
JOKING ASIDE--YOU'VE LIVED THROUGH MOMENTS THE REST OF THE WORLD ONLY READS ABOUT.
I'VE WALKED THE EARTH FOR SO MANY EONS, CHRONICLING MANKIND'S PROGRESS AND EGRESS IS THE ONLY WAY I CAN KEEP TRACK OF LINEAR TIME.
...DO YOU REMEMBER WHEN YOU FIRST 'ARRIVED' ON EARTH?
LONG BEFORE THERE WERE TRINKETS AND NEWSPAPER CLIPPINGS TO COLLECT.

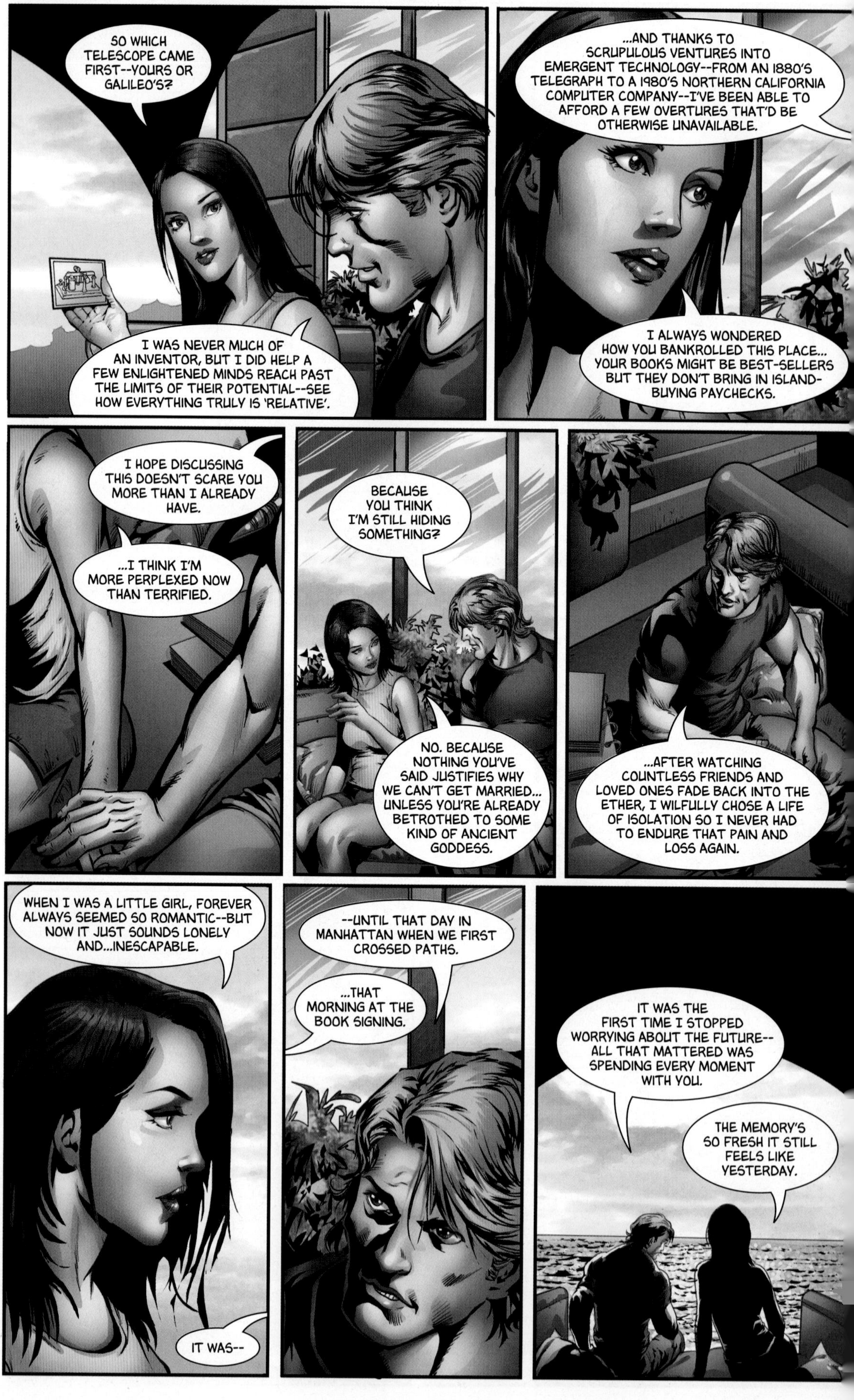
SO WHICH TELESCOPE CAME FIRST--YOURS OR GALILEO'S?
I WAS NEVER MUCH OF AN INVENTOR, BUT I DID HELP A FEW ENLIGHTENED MINDS REACH PAST THE LIMITS OF THEIR POTENTIAL--SEE HOW EVERYTHING TRULY IS 'RELATIVE'.
...AND THANKS TO SCRUPULOUS VENTURES INTO EMERGENT TECHNOLOGY--FROM AN 1880'S TELEGRAPH TO A 1980'S NORTHERN CALIFORNIA COMPUTER COMPANY--I'VE BEEN ABLE TO AFFORD A FEW OVERTURES THAT'D BE OTHERWISE UNAVAILABLE.
I ALWAYS WONDERED HOW YOU BANKROLLED THIS PLACE... YOUR BOOKS MIGHT BE BEST-SELLERS BUT THEY DON'T BRING IN ISLAND-BUYING PAYCHECKS.
I HOPE DISCUSSING THIS DOESN'T SCARE YOU MORE THAN I ALREADY HAVE.
...I THINK I'M MORE PERPLEXED NOW THAN TERRIFIED.
BECAUSE YOU THINK I'M STILL HIDING SOMETHING?
NO. BECAUSE NOTHING YOU'VE SAID JUSTIFIES WHY WE CAN'T GET MARRIED... UNLESS YOU'RE ALREADY BETROTHED TO SOME KIND OF ANCIENT GODDESS.
...AFTER WATCHING COUNTLESS FRIENDS AND LOVED ONES FADE BACK INTO THE ETHER, I WILFULLY CHOSE A LIFE OF ISOLATION SO I NEVER HAD TO ENDURE THAT PAIN AND LOSS AGAIN.
WHEN I WAS A LITTLE GIRL, FOREVER ALWAYS SEEMED SO ROMANTIC--BUT NOW IT JUST SOUNDS LONELY AND...INESCAPABLE.
IT WAS--
--UNTIL THAT DAY IN MANHATTAN WHEN WE FIRST CROSSED PATHS.
...THAT MORNING AT THE BOOK SIGNING.
IT WAS THE FIRST TIME I STOPPED WORRYING ABOUT THE FUTURE--ALL THAT MATTERED WAS SPENDING EVERY MOMENT WITH YOU.
THE MEMORY'S SO FRESH IT STILL FEELS LIKE YESTERDAY.

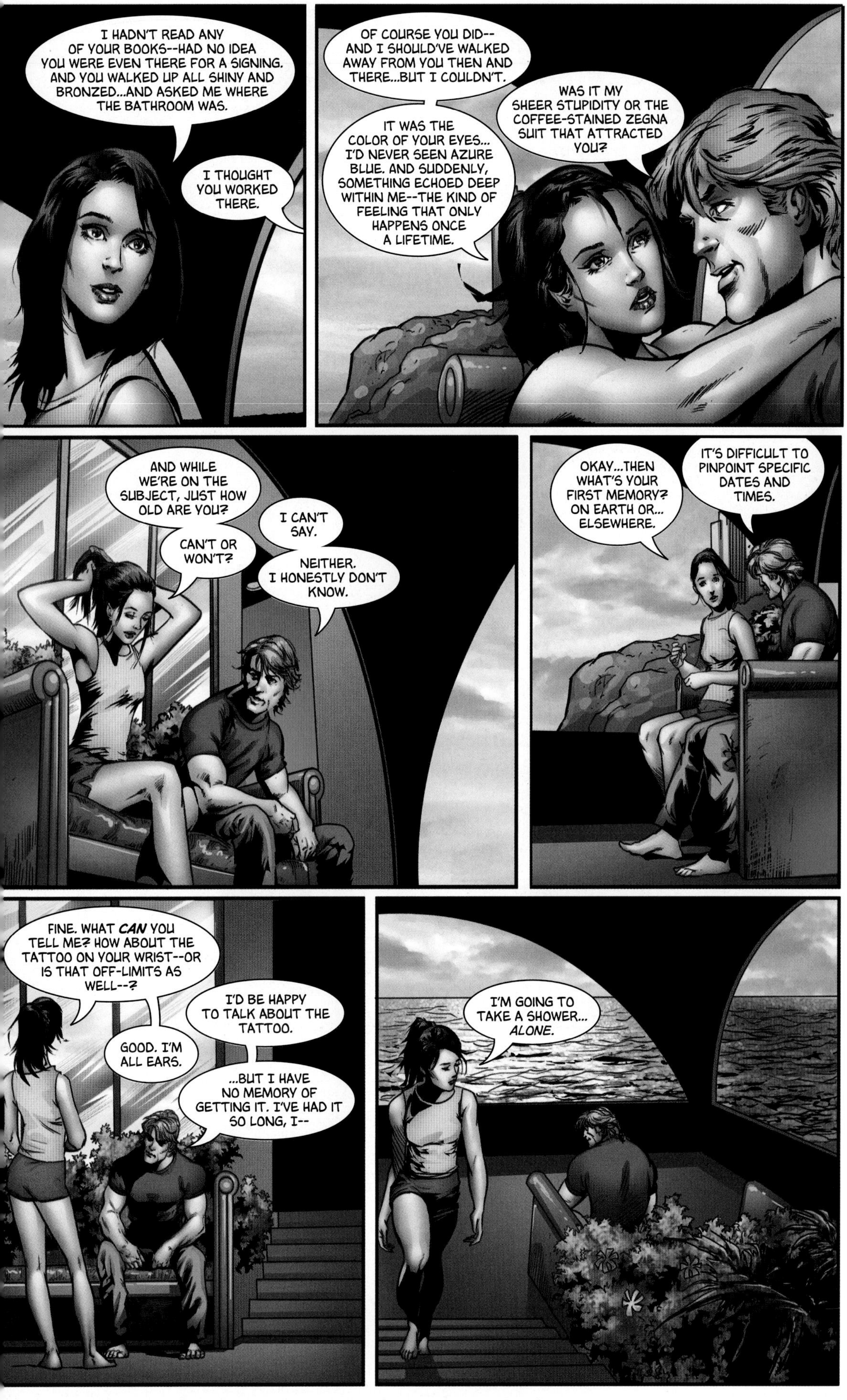

I HADN'T READ ANY OF YOUR BOOKS--HAD NO IDEA YOU WERE EVEN THERE FOR A SIGNING. AND YOU WALKED UP ALL SHINY AND BRONZED...AND ASKED ME WHERE THE BATHROOM WAS.
I THOUGHT YOU WORKED THERE.
OF COURSE YOU DID--AND I SHOULD'VE WALKED AWAY FROM YOU THEN AND THERE...BUT I COULDN'T.
IT WAS THE COLOR OF YOUR EYES... I'D NEVER SEEN AZURE BLUE. AND SUDDENLY, SOMETHING ECHOED DEEP WITHIN ME--THE KIND OF FEELING THAT ONLY HAPPENS ONCE A LIFETIME.
WAS IT MY SHEER STUPIDITY OR THE COFFEE-STAINED ZEGNA SUIT THAT ATTRACTED YOU?
AND WHILE WE'RE ON THE SUBJECT, JUST HOW OLD ARE YOU?
I CAN'T SAY.
CAN'T OR WON'T?
NEITHER. I HONESTLY DON'T KNOW.
OKAY...THEN WHAT'S YOUR FIRST MEMORY? ON EARTH OR... ELSEWHERE.
IT'S DIFFICULT TO PINPOINT SPECIFIC DATES AND TIMES.
FINE. WHAT *CAN* YOU TELL ME? HOW ABOUT THE TATTOO ON YOUR WRIST--OR IS THAT OFF-LIMITS AS WELL--?
I'D BE HAPPY TO TALK ABOUT THE TATTOO.
GOOD. I'M ALL EARS.
...BUT I HAVE NO MEMORY OF GETTING IT. I'VE HAD IT SO LONG, I--
I'M GOING TO TAKE A SHOWER... *ALONE.*

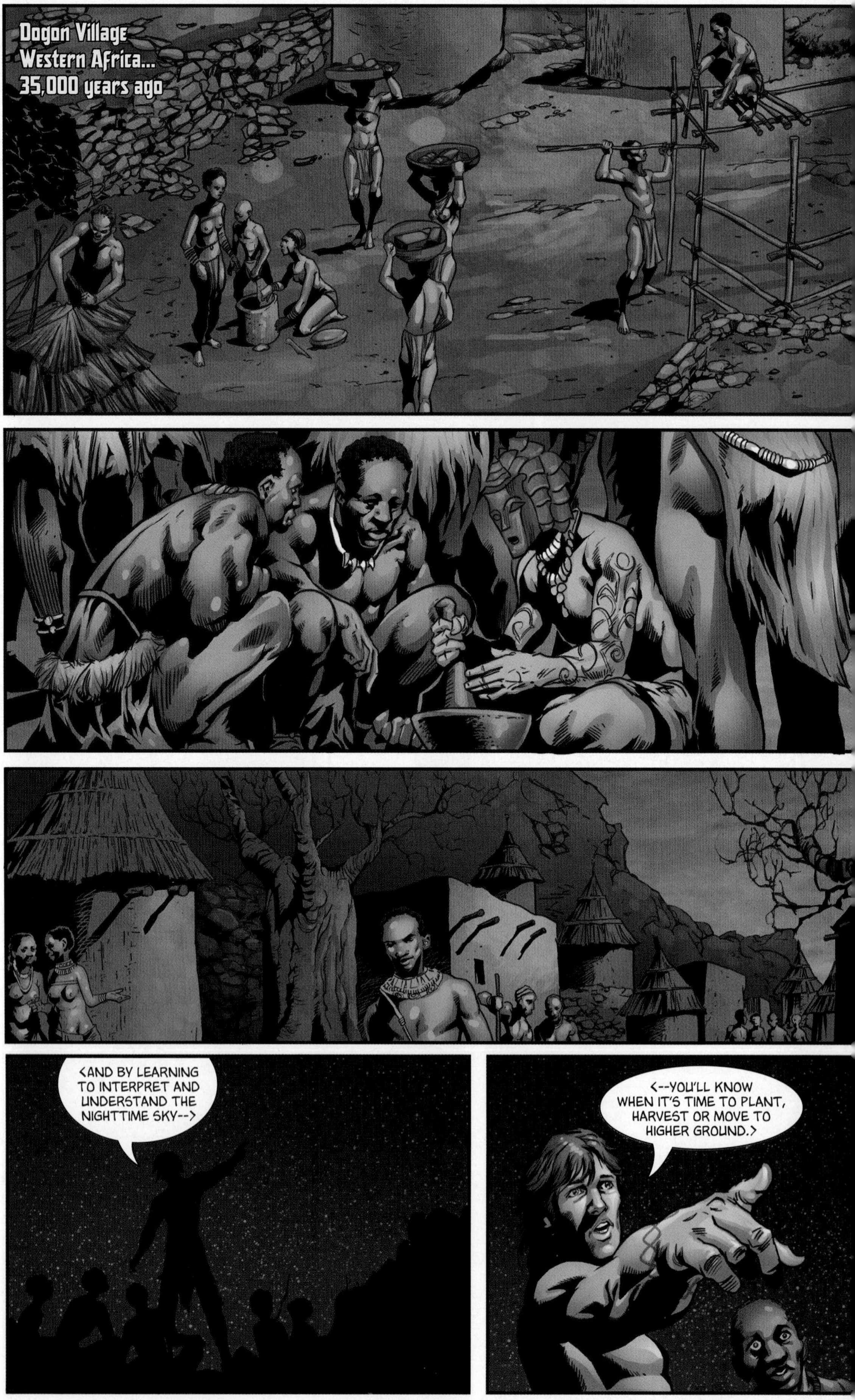
Dogon Village
Western Africa...
35,000 years ago
<AND BY LEARNING TO INTERPRET AND UNDERSTAND THE NIGHTTIME SKY-->
<--YOU'LL KNOW WHEN IT'S TIME TO PLANT, HARVEST OR MOVE TO HIGHER GROUND.>

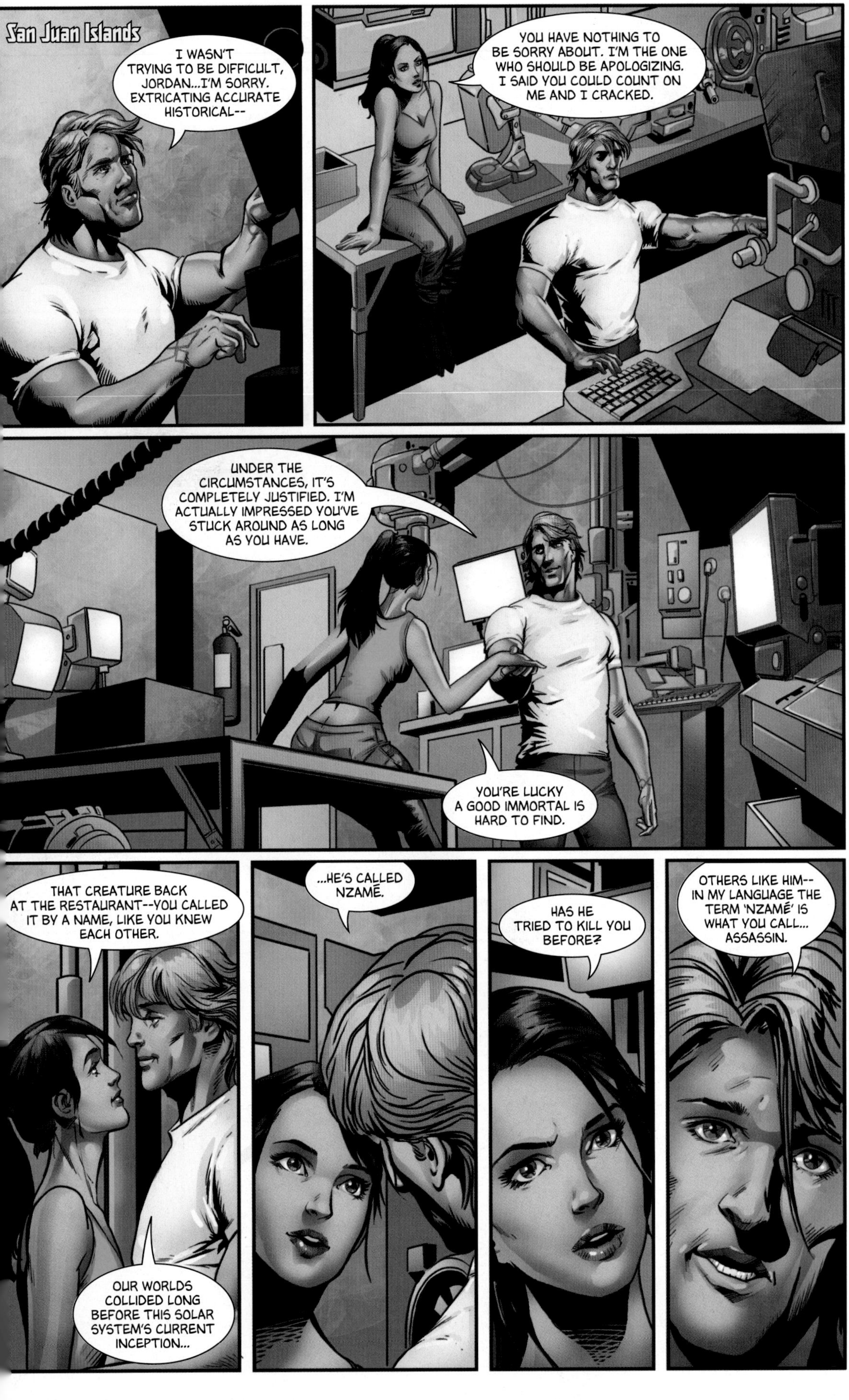
San Juan Islands
I WASN'T TRYING TO BE DIFFICULT, JORDAN...I'M SORRY. EXTRICATING ACCURATE HISTORICAL--
YOU HAVE NOTHING TO BE SORRY ABOUT. I'M THE ONE WHO SHOULD BE APOLOGIZING. I SAID YOU COULD COUNT ON ME AND I CRACKED.
UNDER THE CIRCUMSTANCES, IT'S COMPLETELY JUSTIFIED. I'M ACTUALLY IMPRESSED YOU'VE STUCK AROUND AS LONG AS YOU HAVE.
YOU'RE LUCKY A GOOD IMMORTAL IS HARD TO FIND.
THAT CREATURE BACK AT THE RESTAURANT--YOU CALLED IT BY A NAME, LIKE YOU KNEW EACH OTHER.
OUR WORLDS COLLIDED LONG BEFORE THIS SOLAR SYSTEM'S CURRENT INCEPTION...
...HE'S CALLED NZAMÉ.
HAS HE TRIED TO KILL YOU BEFORE?
OTHERS LIKE HIM-- IN MY LANGUAGE THE TERM 'NZAMÉ' IS WHAT YOU CALL... ASSASSIN.

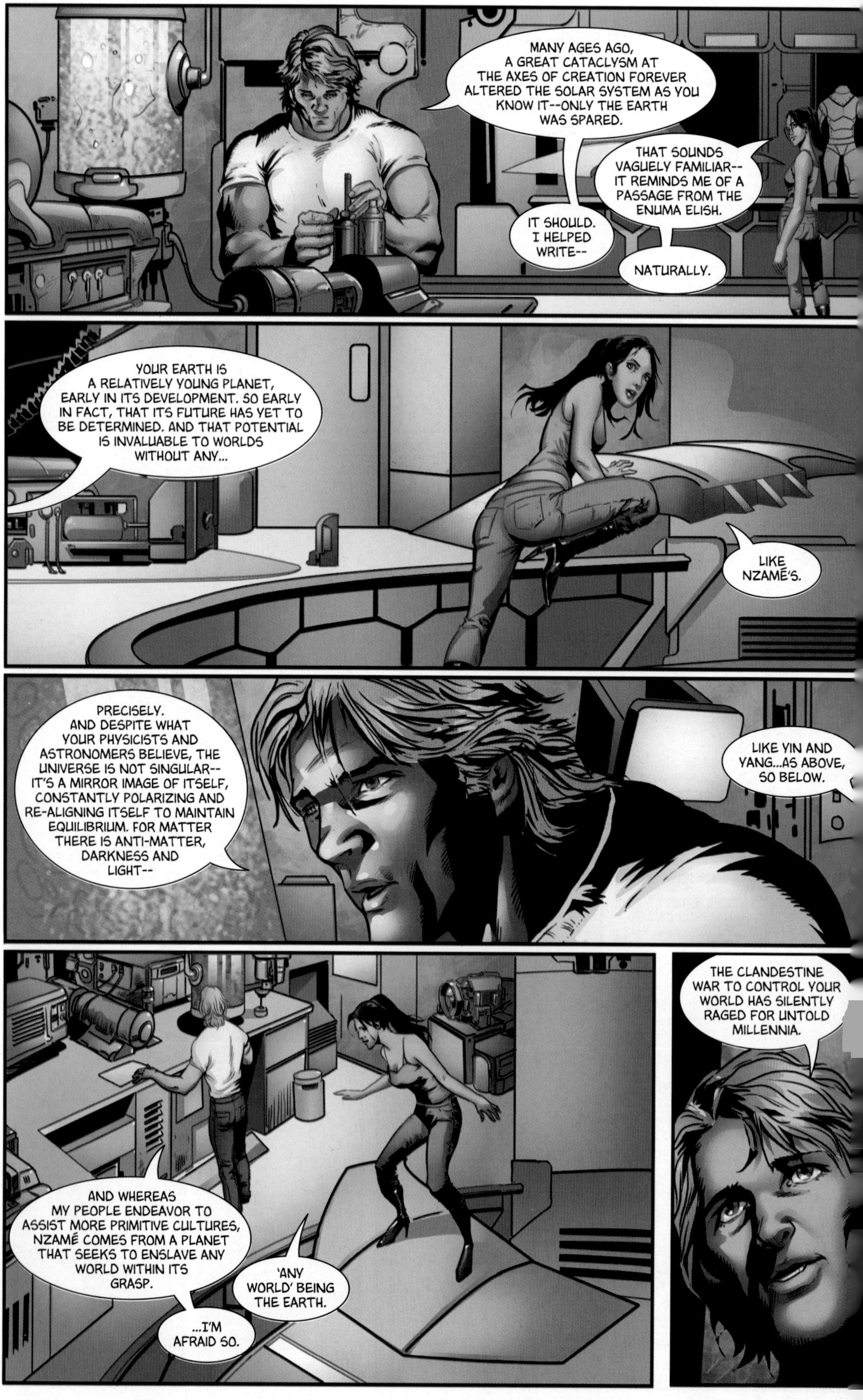
MANY AGES AGO, A GREAT CATACLYSM AT THE AXES OF CREATION FOREVER ALTERED THE SOLAR SYSTEM AS YOU KNOW IT--ONLY THE EARTH WAS SPARED.
THAT SOUNDS VAGUELY FAMILIAR--IT REMINDS ME OF A PASSAGE FROM THE ENUMA ELISH.
IT SHOULD. I HELPED WRITE--
NATURALLY.
YOUR EARTH IS A RELATIVELY YOUNG PLANET, EARLY IN ITS DEVELOPMENT. SO EARLY IN FACT, THAT ITS FUTURE HAS YET TO BE DETERMINED. AND THAT POTENTIAL IS INVALUABLE TO WORLDS WITHOUT ANY...
LIKE NZAMÉ'S.
PRECISELY. AND DESPITE WHAT YOUR PHYSICISTS AND ASTRONOMERS BELIEVE, THE UNIVERSE IS NOT SINGULAR--IT'S A MIRROR IMAGE OF ITSELF, CONSTANTLY POLARIZING AND RE-ALIGNING ITSELF TO MAINTAIN EQUILIBRIUM. FOR MATTER THERE IS ANTI-MATTER, DARKNESS AND LIGHT--
LIKE YIN AND YANG...AS ABOVE, SO BELOW.
AND WHEREAS MY PEOPLE ENDEAVOR TO ASSIST MORE PRIMITIVE CULTURES, NZAMÉ COMES FROM A PLANET THAT SEEKS TO ENSLAVE ANY WORLD WITHIN ITS GRASP.
'ANY WORLD' BEING THE EARTH.
...I'M AFRAID SO.
THE CLANDESTINE WAR TO CONTROL YOUR WORLD HAS SILENTLY RAGED FOR UNTOLD MILLENNIA.

HOW MANY 'SENTINELS' ARE STILL STATIONED HERE?

WE LOST CONTACT AFTER WE WERE FORCED UNDERGROUND SO IT'S DIFFICULT TO SAY.

YOU WENT INTO HIDING?

IN THE DAYS BEFORE THE CONTINENTS SEPARATED, OUR NUMBERS WERE PLENTIFUL AND THE PRIMITIVE ABORIGINAL TRIBES WORSHIPPED US. WE LIVED PEACEFULLY, INTERCONNECTED WITH THE SOIL OF THE EARTH AND THE WATER OF ITS OCEANS--UNTIL NZAMÉ'S PLANET STARTED ITS MASSACRE.

THE FEW WHO ESCAPED FOUND THEMSELVES CONSCRIPTED TO ETERNAL EXILE ON A WORLD THAT HARDLY KNEW THEY EXISTED...SO WE AGREED TO DISAPPEAR UNNOTICED INTO THE EVOLVING CIVILIZATIONS AND SOCIETIES AROUND THE WORLD.

...THEN YOU HAVE NO WAY OF KNOWING IF ANY OF YOUR PEOPLE ARE LEFT?

SOME...I'M UNSURE HOW MANY ARE STILL ALIVE BUT I ALWAYS KNOW WHEN ONE OF US DIES.

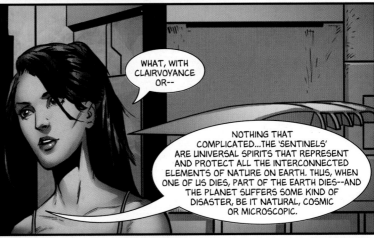

WHAT, WITH CLAIRVOYANCE OR--

NOTHING THAT COMPLICATED...THE 'SENTINELS' ARE UNIVERSAL SPIRITS THAT REPRESENT AND PROTECT ALL THE INTERCONNECTED ELEMENTS OF NATURE ON EARTH. THUS, WHEN ONE OF US DIES, PART OF THE EARTH DIES--AND THE PLANET SUFFERS SOME KIND OF DISASTER, BE IT NATURAL, COSMIC OR MICROSCOPIC.

WHICH MEANS IF THIS NZAMÉ KEEPS KILLING OFF 'SENTINELS'...

THE EARTH'S LIFE-BEARING CAPABILITIES WILL EXPIRE--AND HIS PLANET TAKES CONTROL OF WHAT'S LEFT.

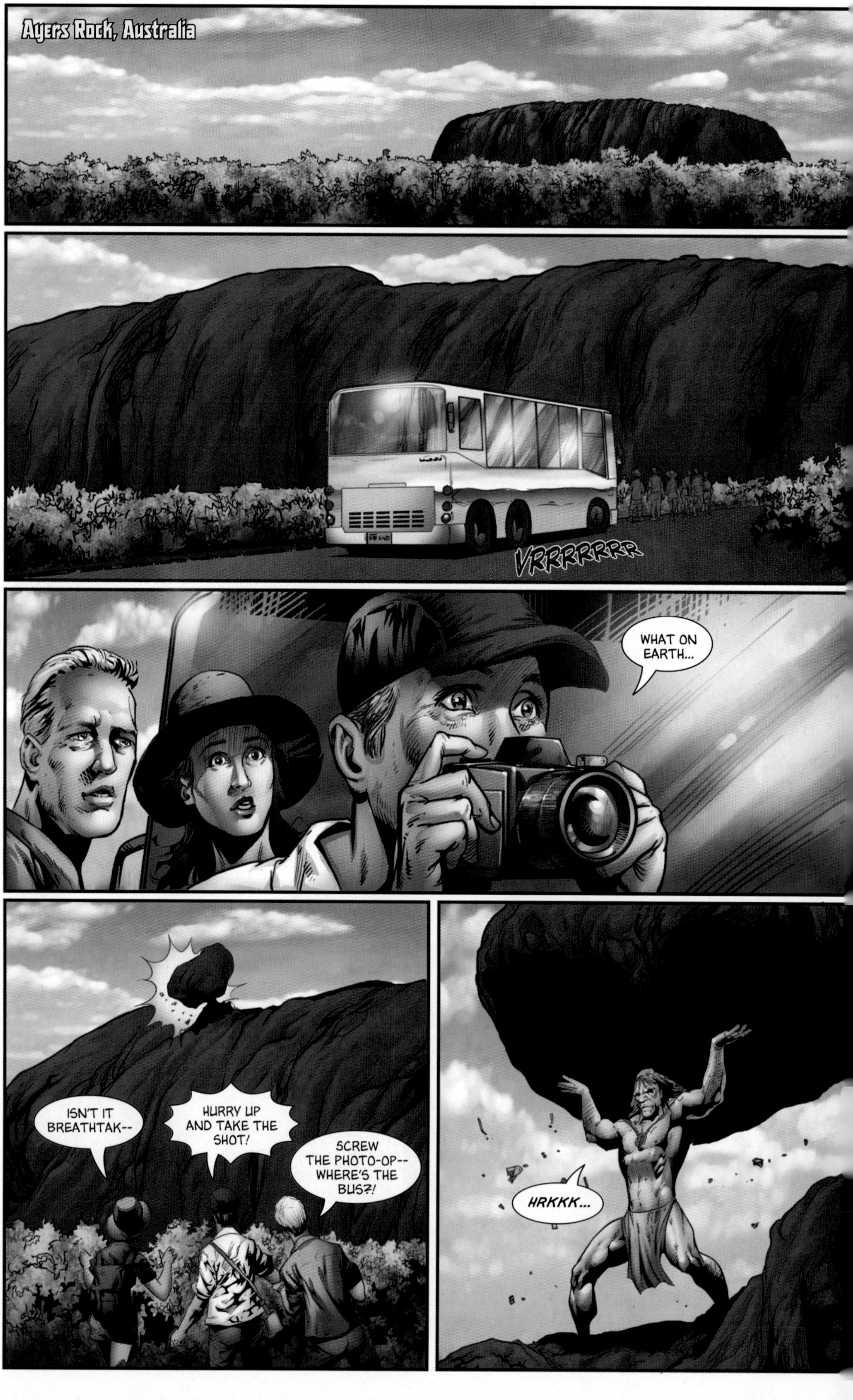

Ayers Rock, Australia
VRRRRRRR
WHAT ON EARTH...
ISN'T IT BREATHTAK--
HURRY UP AND TAKE THE SHOT!
SCREW THE PHOTO-OP-- WHERE'S THE BUS?!
HRKKK...

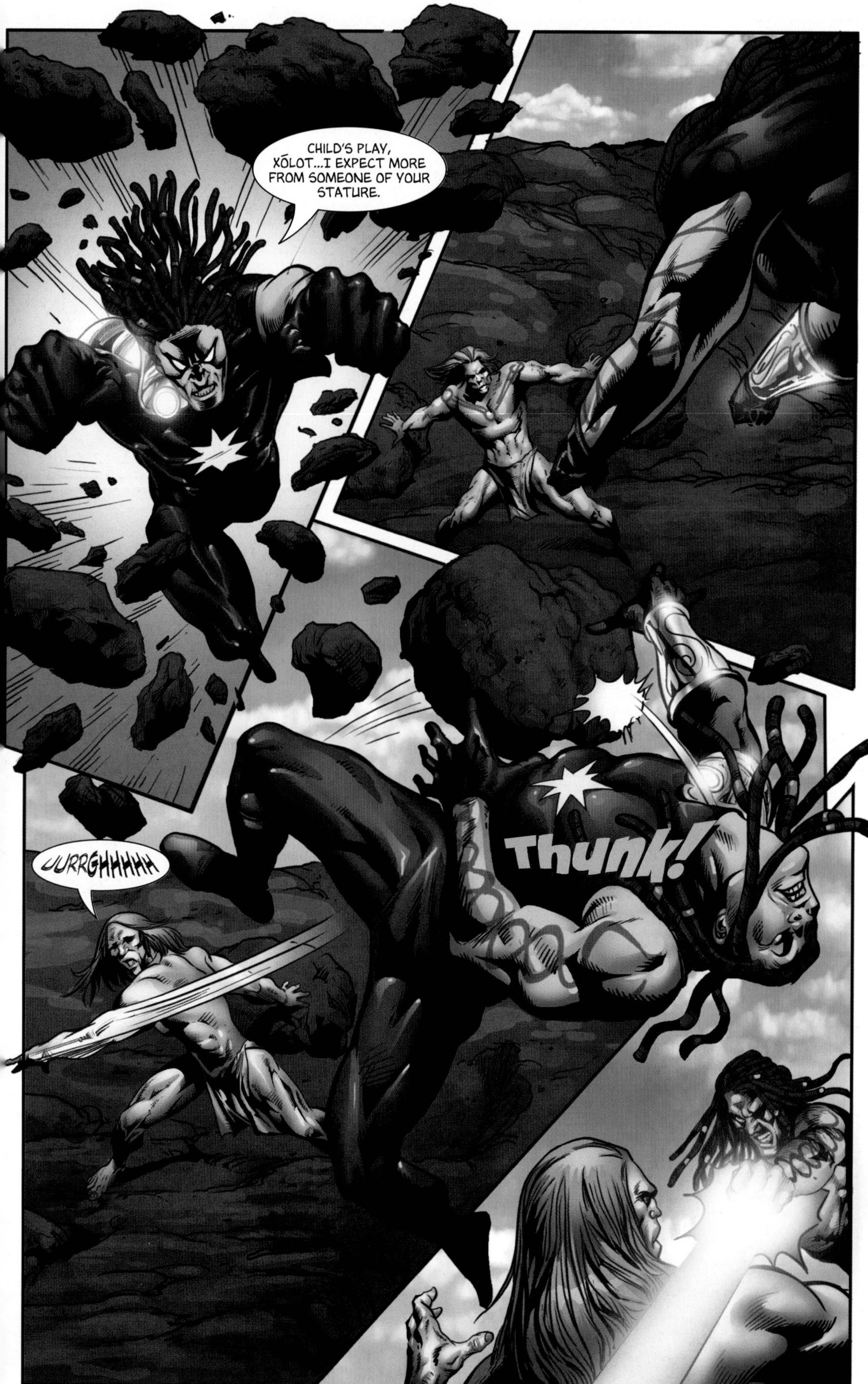
CHILD'S PLAY, XŌLOT...I EXPECT MORE FROM SOMEONE OF YOUR STATURE.
UURRGHHHHH
Thunk!

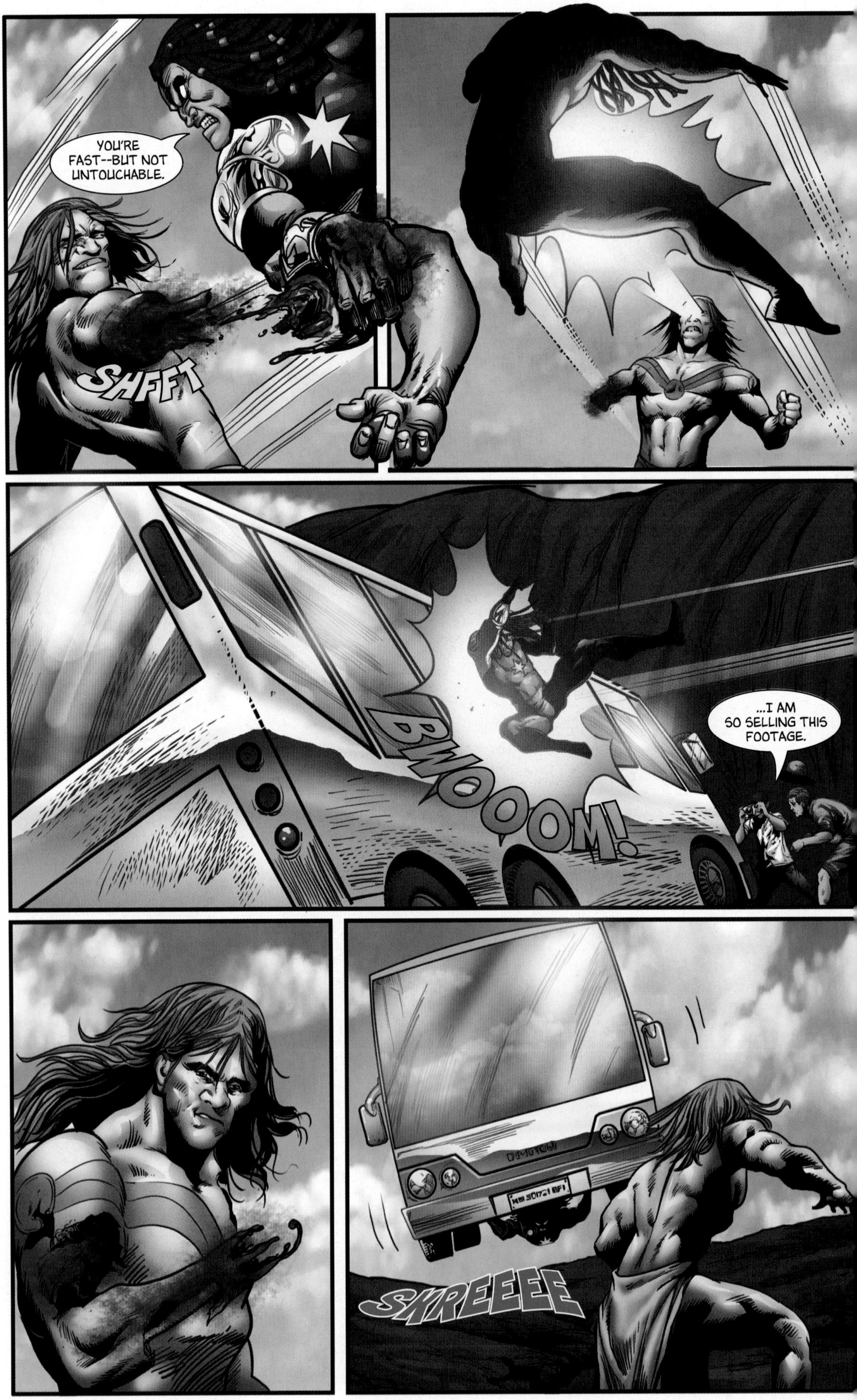
YOU'RE FAST--BUT NOT UNTOUCHABLE.
SHFFT
BWOOOOM!
...I AM SO SELLING THIS FOOTAGE.
SKREEEE

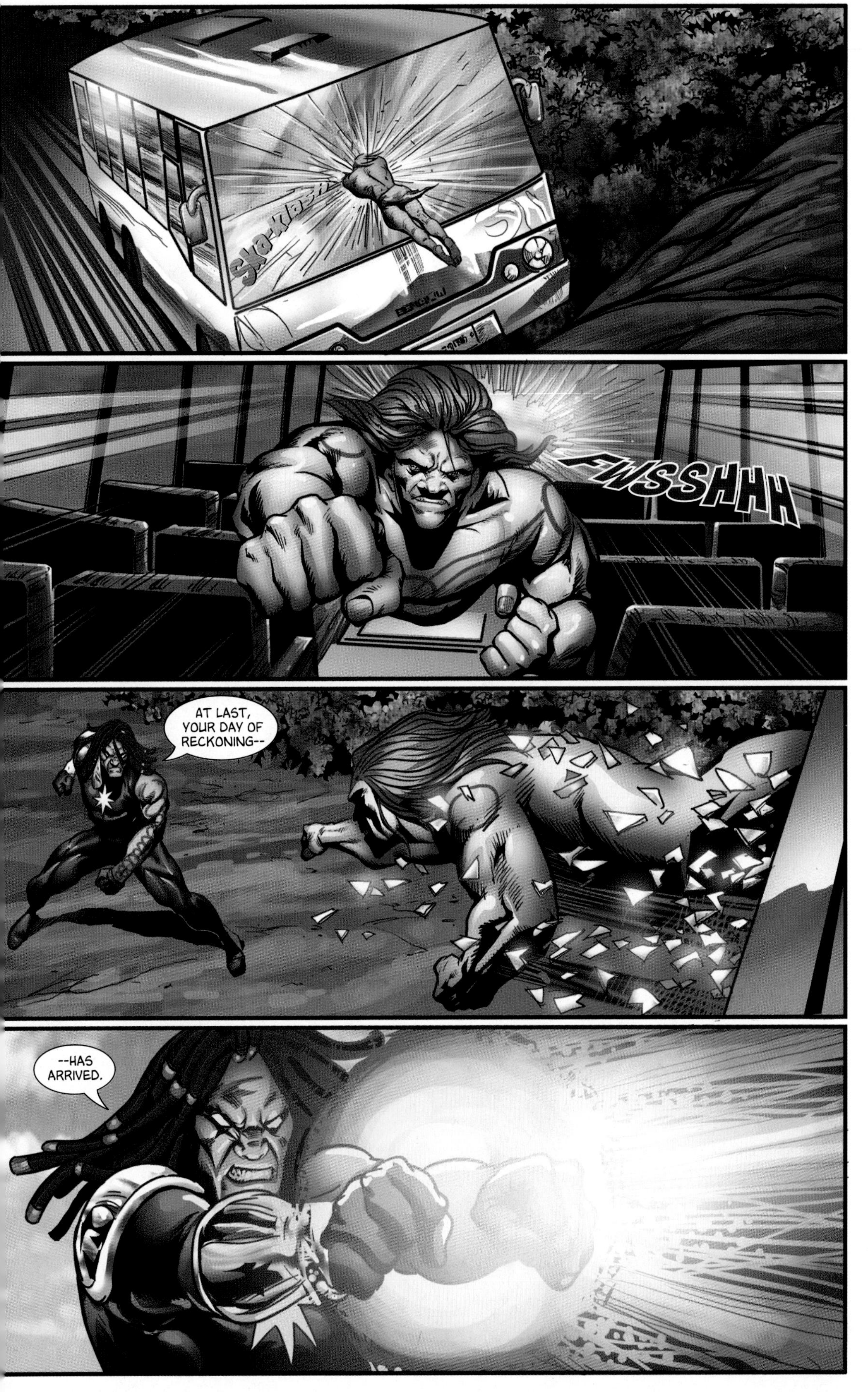
Ska-Klash
FWSSHHH
AT LAST, YOUR DAY OF RECKONING--
--HAS ARRIVED.

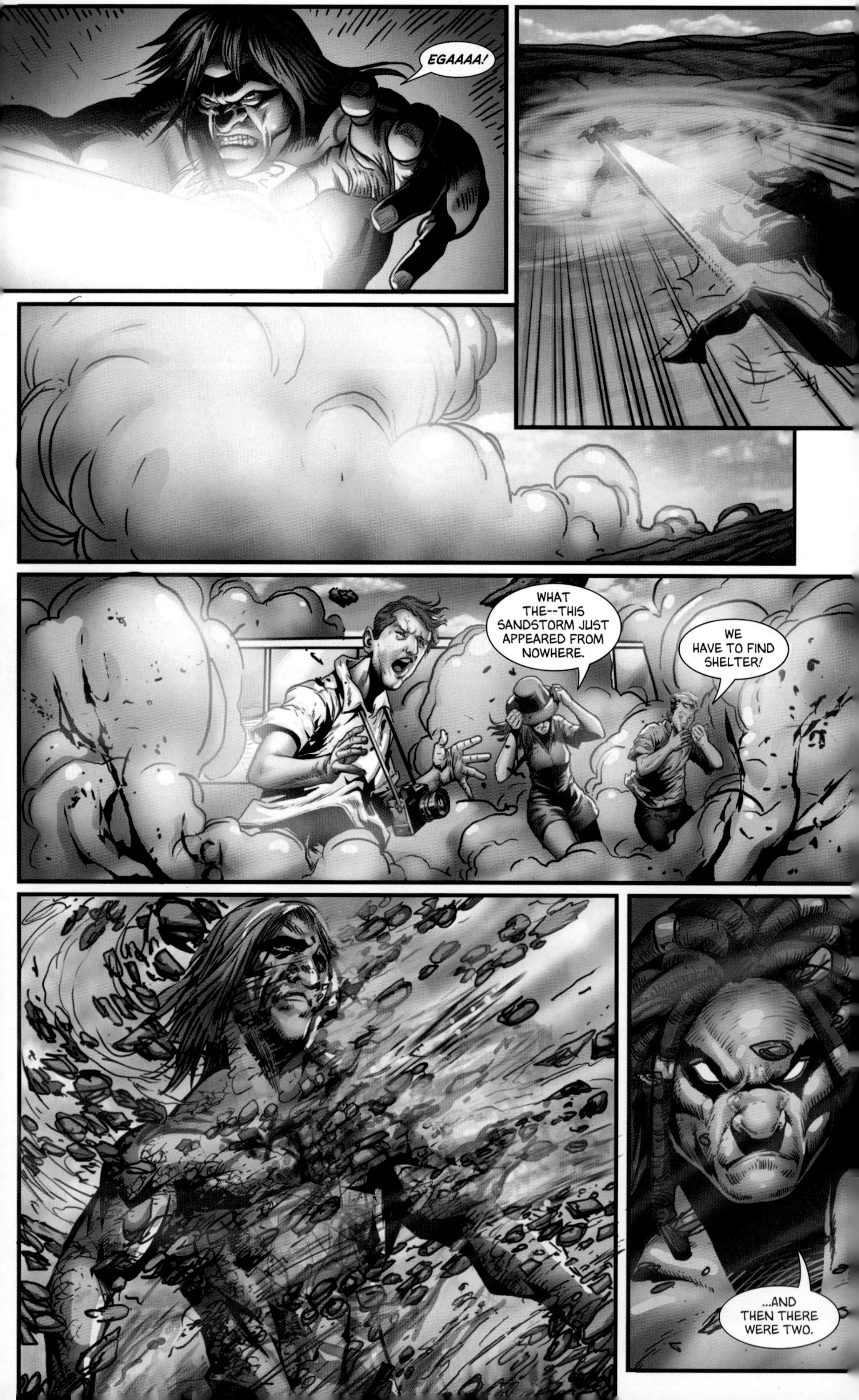
EGAAAA!
WHAT THE--THIS SANDSTORM JUST APPEARED FROM NOWHERE.
WE HAVE TO FIND SHELTER!
...AND THEN THERE WERE TWO.

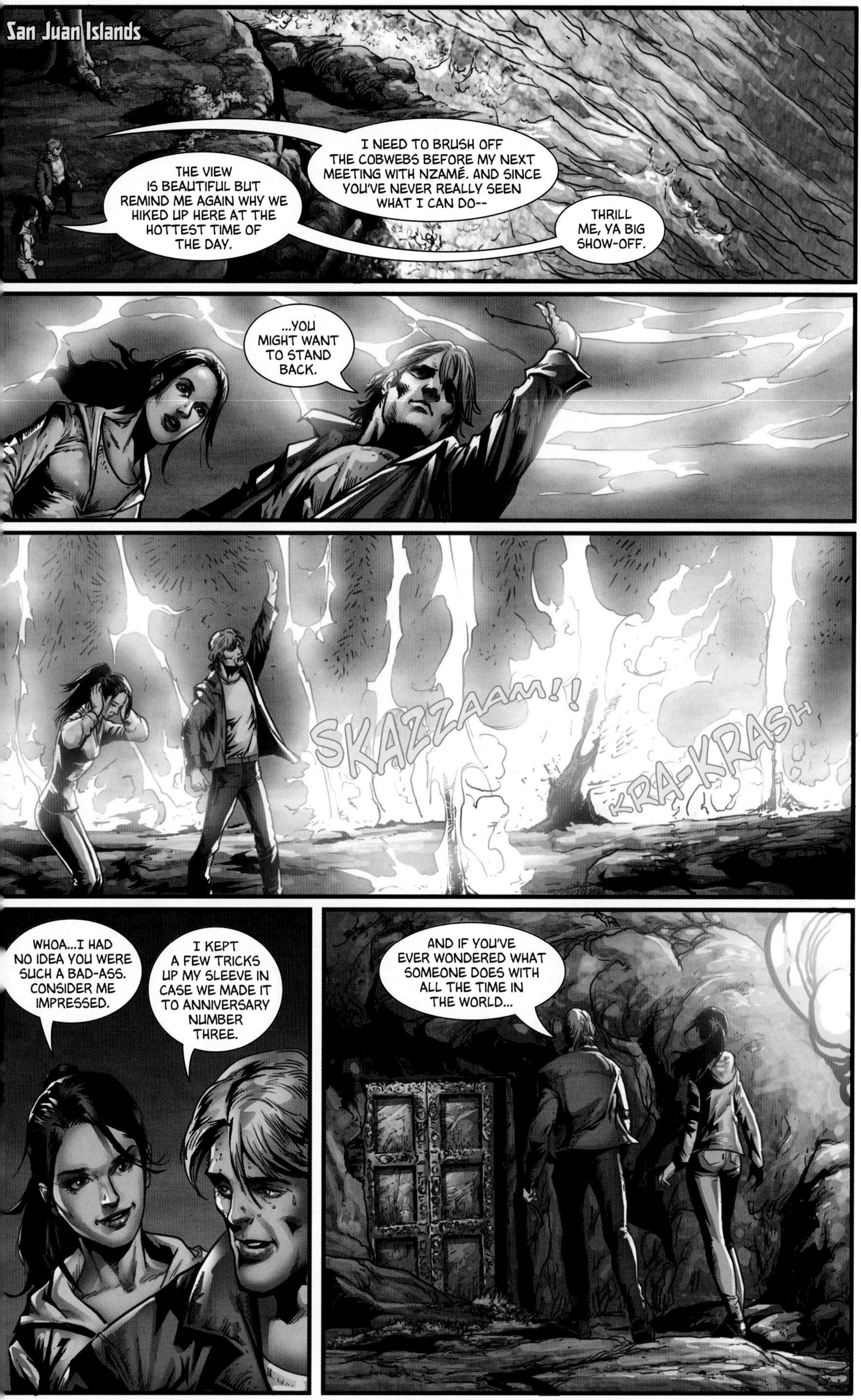

San Juan Islands
THE VIEW IS BEAUTIFUL BUT REMIND ME AGAIN WHY WE HIKED UP HERE AT THE HOTTEST TIME OF THE DAY.
I NEED TO BRUSH OFF THE COBWEBS BEFORE MY NEXT MEETING WITH NZAMÉ. AND SINCE YOU'VE NEVER REALLY SEEN WHAT I CAN DO--
THRILL ME, YA BIG SHOW-OFF.
...YOU MIGHT WANT TO STAND BACK.
SKAZZAAM!!
KRA-KRASH
WHOA...I HAD NO IDEA YOU WERE SUCH A BAD-ASS. CONSIDER ME IMPRESSED.
I KEPT A FEW TRICKS UP MY SLEEVE IN CASE WE MADE IT TO ANNIVERSARY NUMBER THREE.
AND IF YOU'VE EVER WONDERED WHAT SOMEONE DOES WITH ALL THE TIME IN THE WORLD...

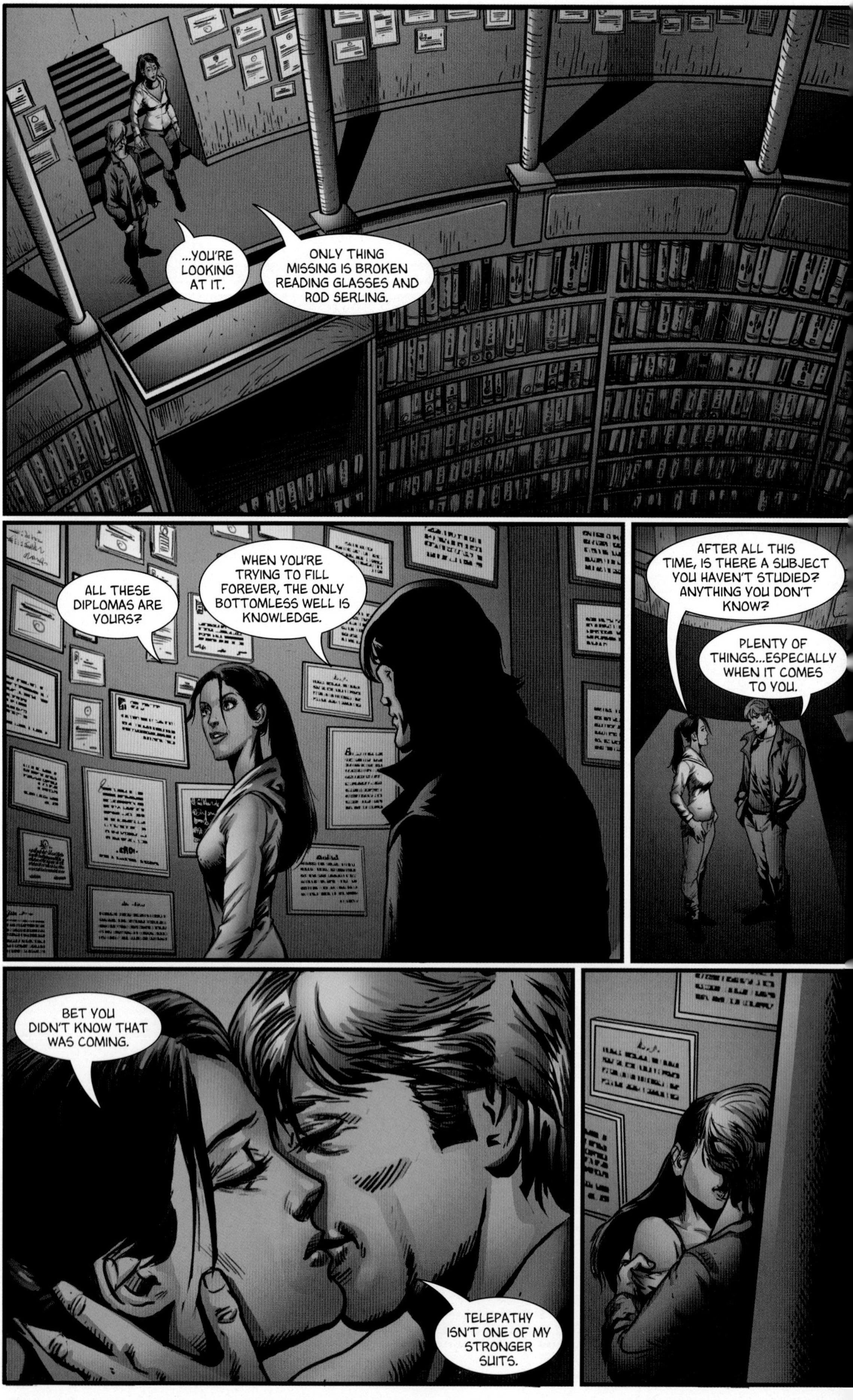
...YOU'RE LOOKING AT IT.
ONLY THING MISSING IS BROKEN READING GLASSES AND ROD SERLING.
ALL THESE DIPLOMAS ARE YOURS?
WHEN YOU'RE TRYING TO FILL FOREVER, THE ONLY BOTTOMLESS WELL IS KNOWLEDGE.
AFTER ALL THIS TIME, IS THERE A SUBJECT YOU HAVEN'T STUDIED? ANYTHING YOU DON'T KNOW?
PLENTY OF THINGS...ESPECIALLY WHEN IT COMES TO YOU.
BET YOU DIDN'T KNOW THAT WAS COMING.
TELEPATHY ISN'T ONE OF MY STRONGER SUITS.

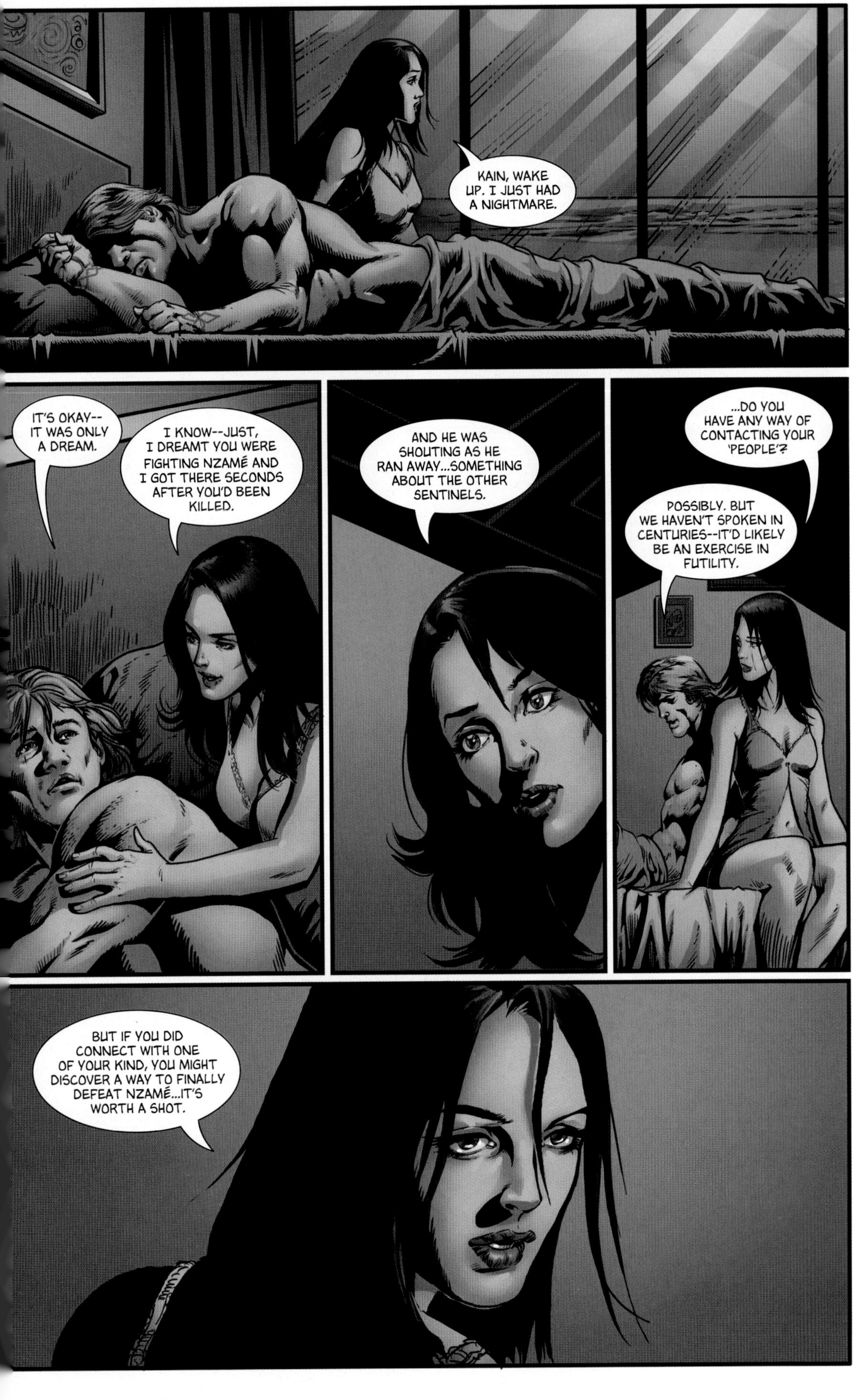
KAIN, WAKE UP. I JUST HAD A NIGHTMARE.
IT'S OKAY-- IT WAS ONLY A DREAM.
I KNOW--JUST, I DREAMT YOU WERE FIGHTING NZAMÉ AND I GOT THERE SECONDS AFTER YOU'D BEEN KILLED.
AND HE WAS SHOUTING AS HE RAN AWAY...SOMETHING ABOUT THE OTHER SENTINELS.
...DO YOU HAVE ANY WAY OF CONTACTING YOUR 'PEOPLE'?
POSSIBLY. BUT WE HAVEN'T SPOKEN IN CENTURIES--IT'D LIKELY BE AN EXERCISE IN FUTILITY.
BUT IF YOU DID CONNECT WITH ONE OF YOUR KIND, YOU MIGHT DISCOVER A WAY TO FINALLY DEFEAT NZAMÉ...IT'S WORTH A SHOT.

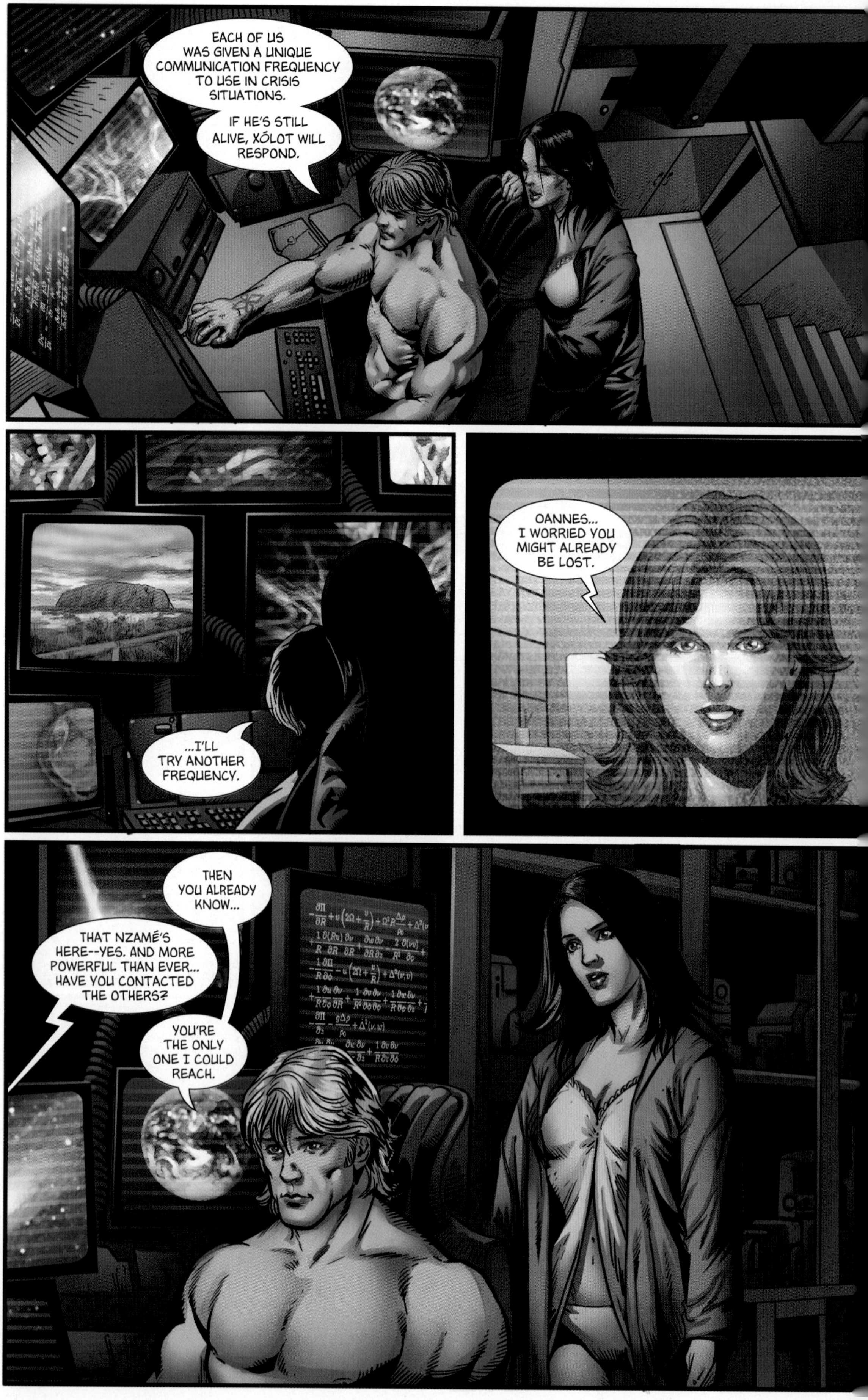
EACH OF US WAS GIVEN A UNIQUE COMMUNICATION FREQUENCY TO USE IN CRISIS SITUATIONS.
IF HE'S STILL ALIVE, XÓLOT WILL RESPOND.
...I'LL TRY ANOTHER FREQUENCY.
OANNES... I WORRIED YOU MIGHT ALREADY BE LOST.
THEN YOU ALREADY KNOW...
THAT NZAMÉ'S HERE--YES. AND MORE POWERFUL THAN EVER... HAVE YOU CONTACTED THE OTHERS?
YOU'RE THE ONLY ONE I COULD REACH.

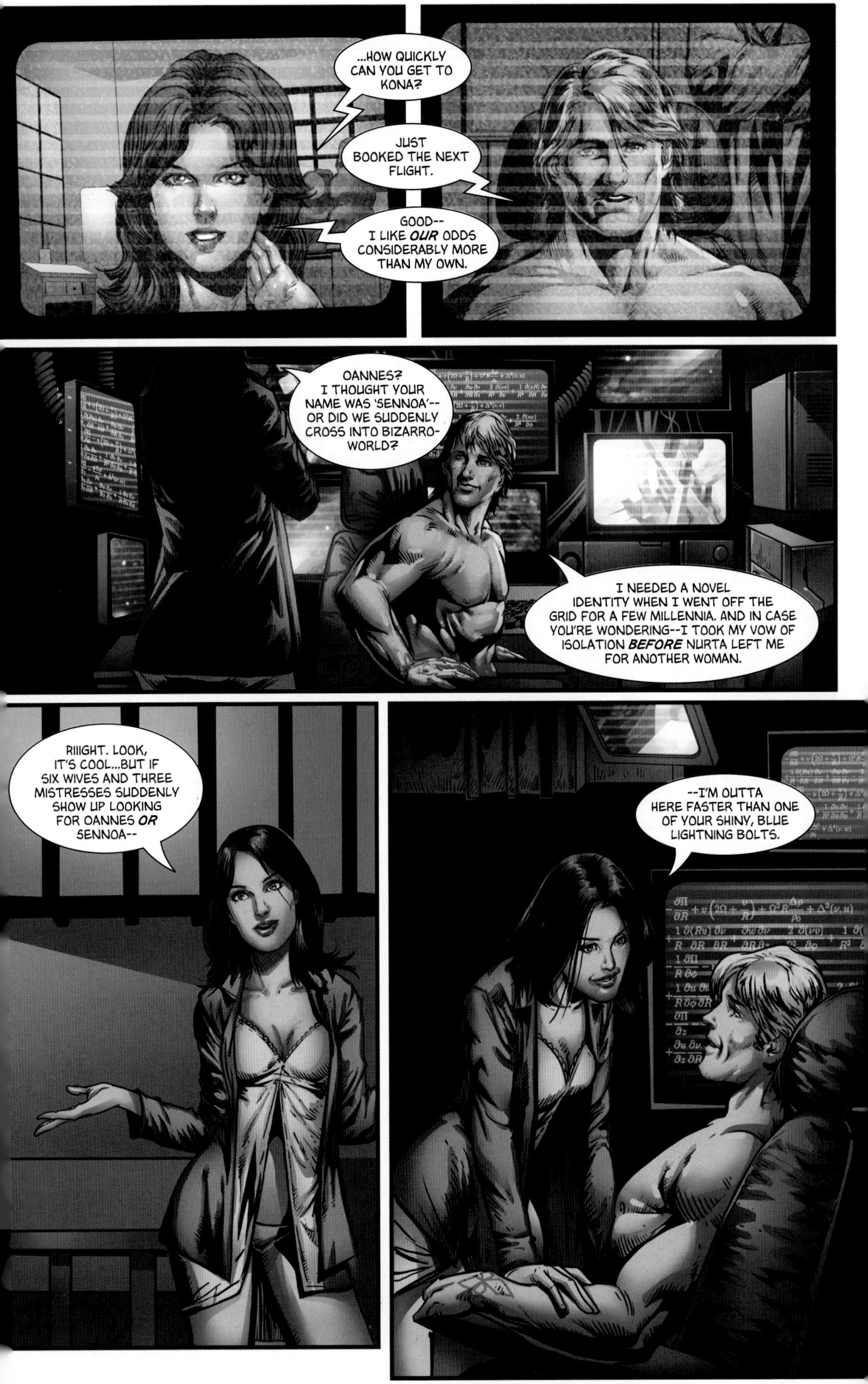

...HOW QUICKLY CAN YOU GET TO KONA?
JUST BOOKED THE NEXT FLIGHT.
GOOD-- I LIKE ***OUR*** ODDS CONSIDERABLY MORE THAN MY OWN.
OANNES? I THOUGHT YOUR NAME WAS 'SENNOA'-- OR DID WE SUDDENLY CROSS INTO BIZARRO-WORLD?
I NEEDED A NOVEL IDENTITY WHEN I WENT OFF THE GRID FOR A FEW MILLENNIA. AND IN CASE YOU'RE WONDERING--I TOOK MY VOW OF ISOLATION ***BEFORE*** NURTA LEFT ME FOR ANOTHER WOMAN.
RIIIGHT. LOOK, IT'S COOL...BUT IF SIX WIVES AND THREE MISTRESSES SUDDENLY SHOW UP LOOKING FOR OANNES ***OR*** SENNOA--
--I'M OUTTA HERE FASTER THAN ONE OF YOUR SHINY, BLUE LIGHTNING BOLTS.

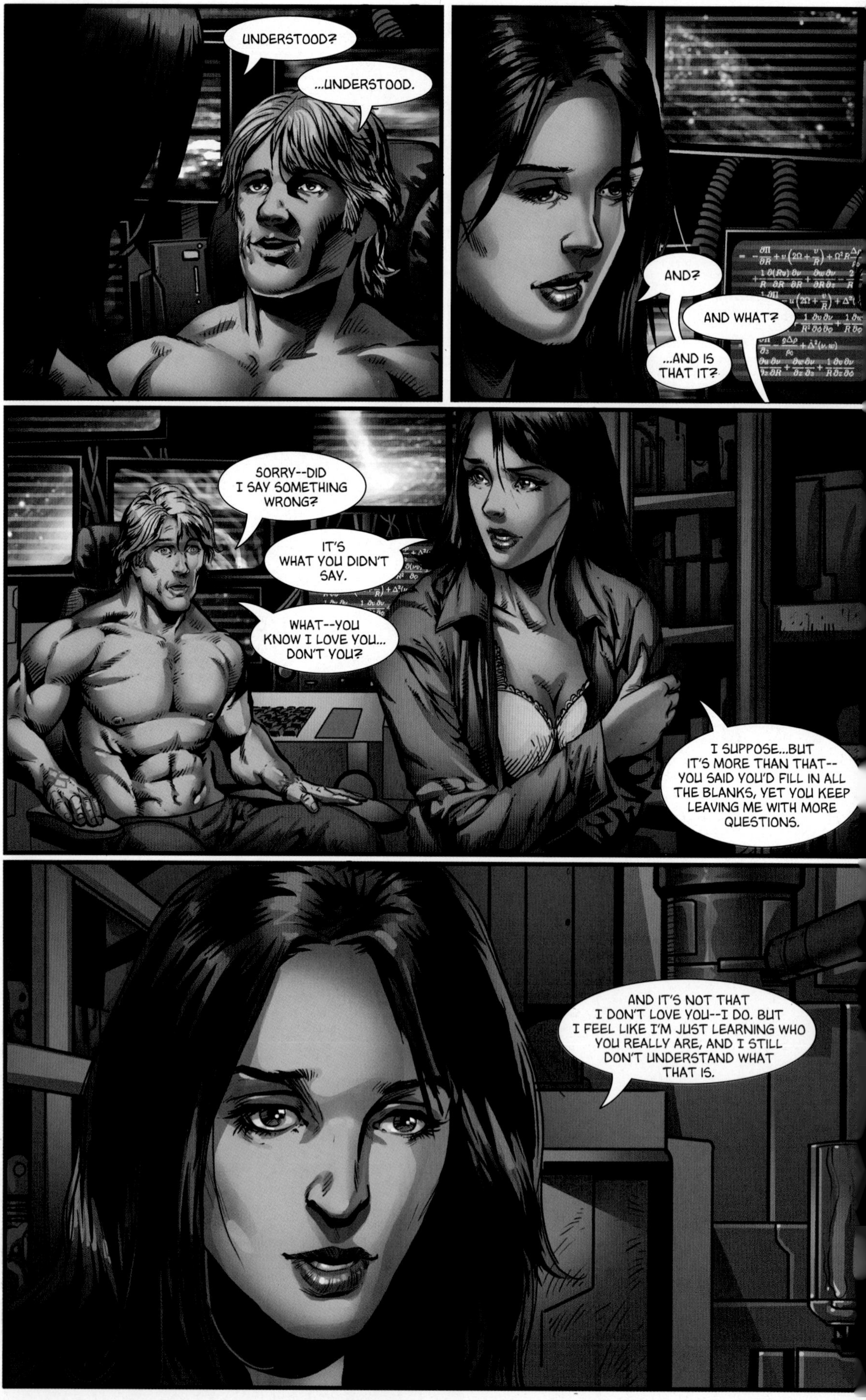
UNDERSTOOD?
...UNDERSTOOD.
AND?
AND WHAT?
...AND IS THAT IT?
SORRY--DID I SAY SOMETHING WRONG?
IT'S WHAT YOU DIDN'T SAY.
WHAT--YOU KNOW I LOVE YOU... DON'T YOU?
I SUPPOSE...BUT IT'S MORE THAN THAT--YOU SAID YOU'D FILL IN ALL THE BLANKS, YET YOU KEEP LEAVING ME WITH MORE QUESTIONS.
AND IT'S NOT THAT I DON'T LOVE YOU--I DO. BUT I FEEL LIKE I'M JUST LEARNING WHO YOU REALLY ARE, AND I STILL DON'T UNDERSTAND WHAT THAT IS.

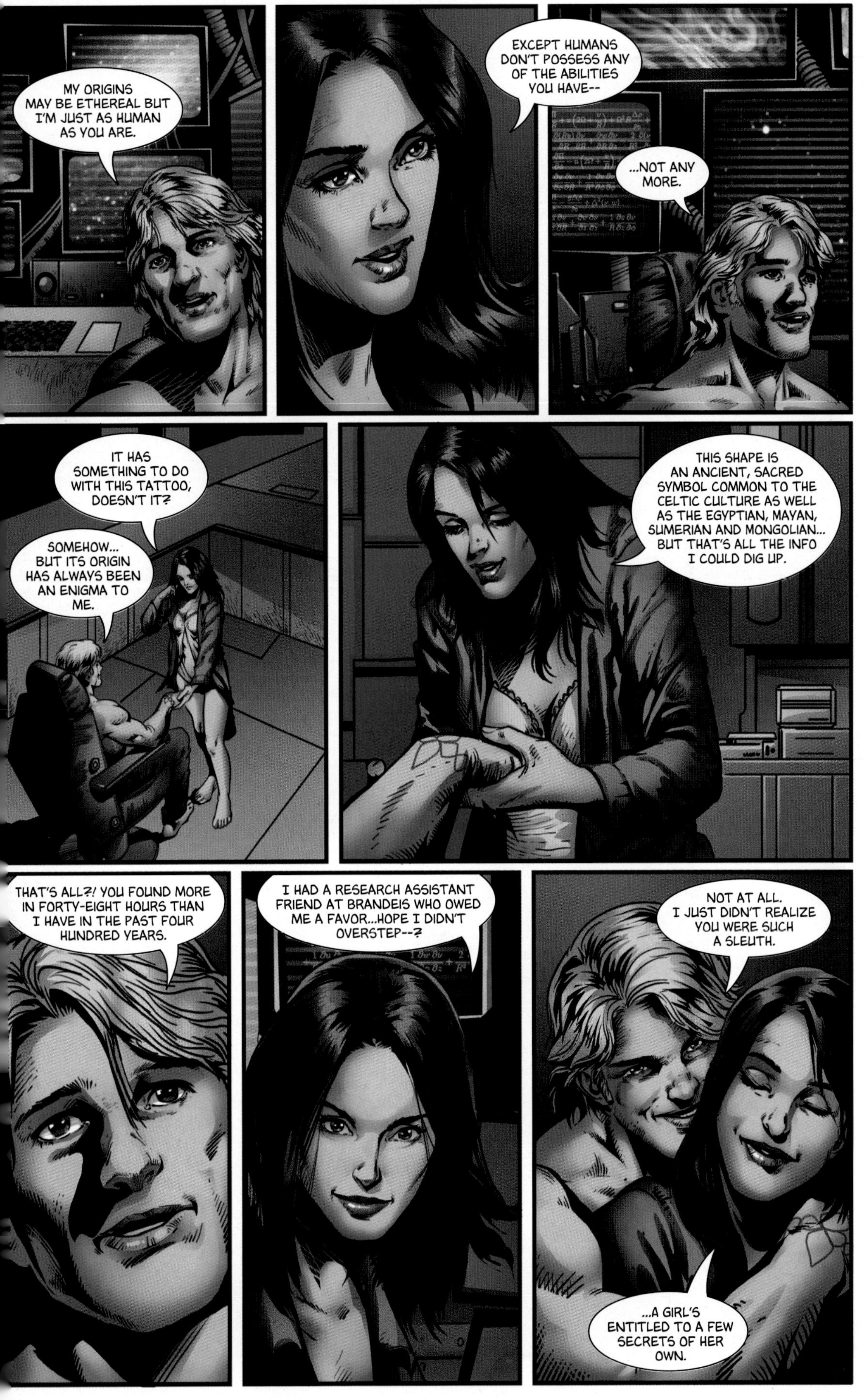
MY ORIGINS MAY BE ETHEREAL BUT I'M JUST AS HUMAN AS YOU ARE.
EXCEPT HUMANS DON'T POSSESS ANY OF THE ABILITIES YOU HAVE--
...NOT ANY MORE.
IT HAS SOMETHING TO DO WITH THIS TATTOO, DOESN'T IT?
SOMEHOW... BUT ITS ORIGIN HAS ALWAYS BEEN AN ENIGMA TO ME.
THIS SHAPE IS AN ANCIENT, SACRED SYMBOL COMMON TO THE CELTIC CULTURE AS WELL AS THE EGYPTIAN, MAYAN, SUMERIAN AND MONGOLIAN... BUT THAT'S ALL THE INFO I COULD DIG UP.
THAT'S ALL?! YOU FOUND MORE IN FORTY-EIGHT HOURS THAN I HAVE IN THE PAST FOUR HUNDRED YEARS.
I HAD A RESEARCH ASSISTANT FRIEND AT BRANDEIS WHO OWED ME A FAVOR...HOPE I DIDN'T OVERSTEP--?
NOT AT ALL. I JUST DIDN'T REALIZE YOU WERE SUCH A SLEUTH.
...A GIRL'S ENTITLED TO A FEW SECRETS OF HER OWN.

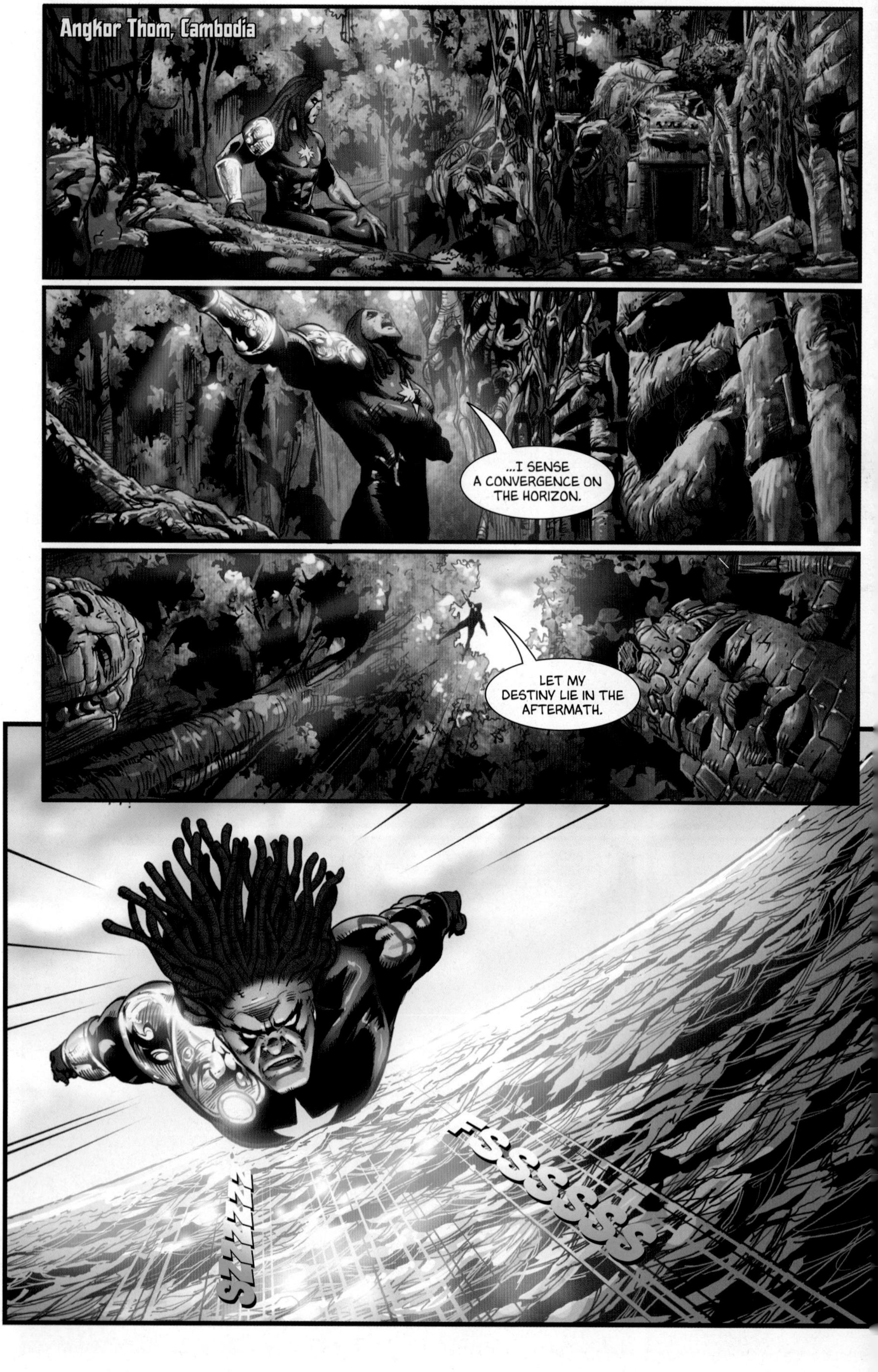
Angkor Thom, Cambodia
...I SENSE A CONVERGENCE ON THE HORIZON.
LET MY DESTINY LIE IN THE AFTERMATH.
FSSSSSS
SZZZZZZ

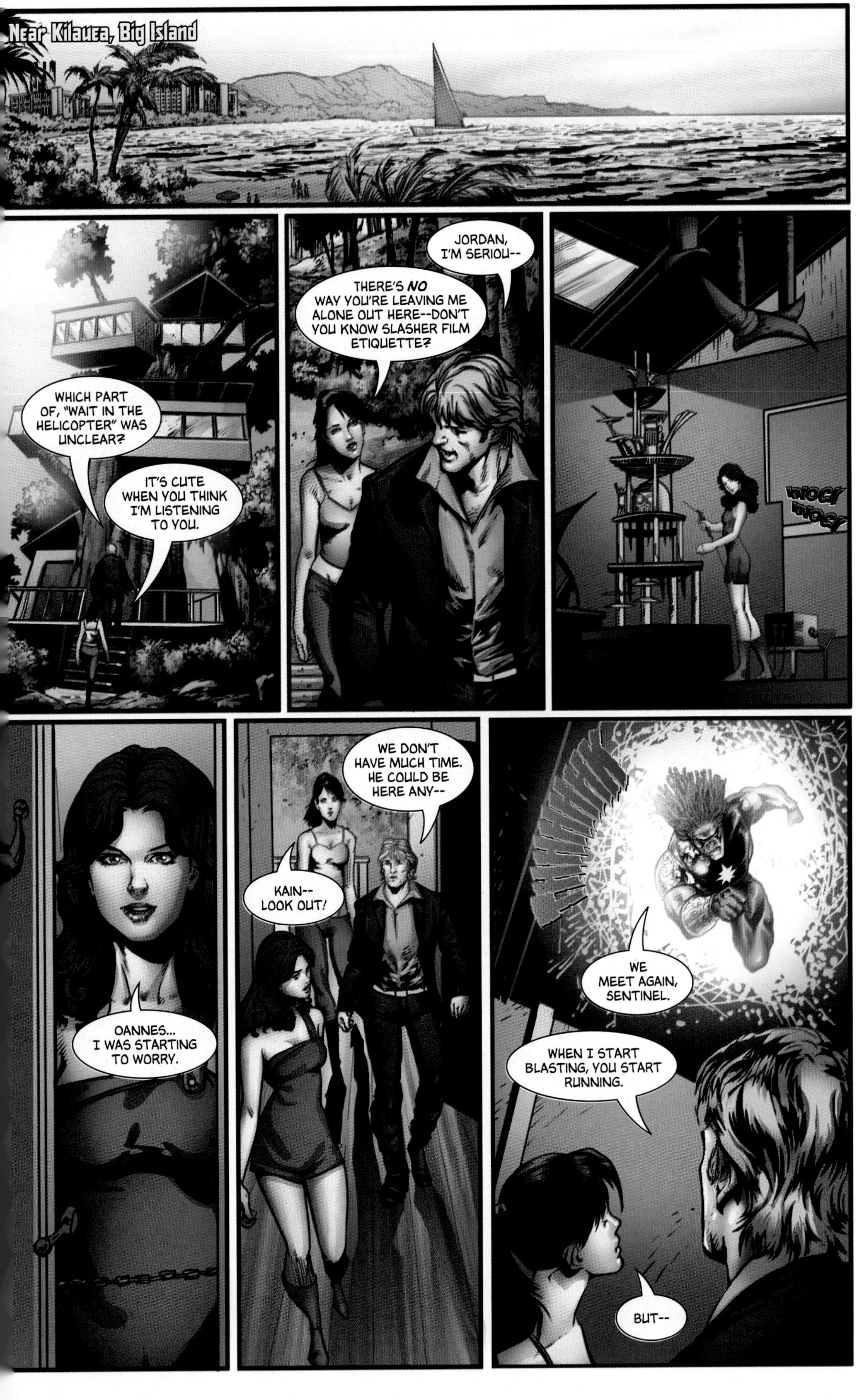
Near Kilauea, Big Island
WHICH PART OF, "WAIT IN THE HELICOPTER" WAS UNCLEAR?
IT'S CUTE WHEN YOU THINK I'M LISTENING TO YOU.
JORDAN, I'M SERIOU--
THERE'S ***NO*** WAY YOU'RE LEAVING ME ALONE OUT HERE--DON'T YOU KNOW SLASHER FILM ETIQUETTE?
KNOCK KNOCK
OANNES... I WAS STARTING TO WORRY.
WE DON'T HAVE MUCH TIME. HE COULD BE HERE ANY--
KAIN-- LOOK OUT!
WE MEET AGAIN, SENTINEL.
WHEN I START BLASTING, YOU START RUNNING.
BUT--

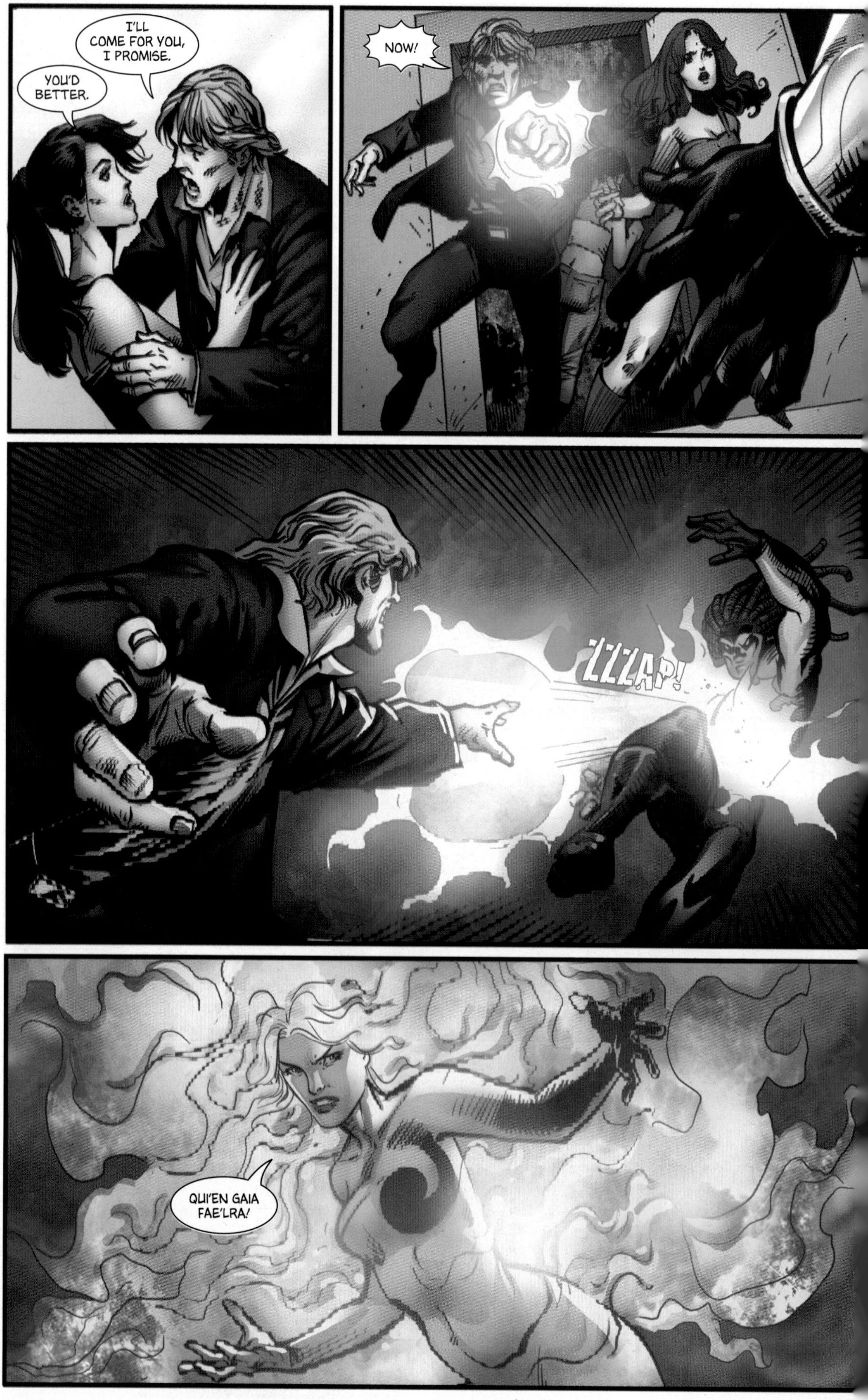
I'LL COME FOR YOU, I PROMISE.
YOU'D BETTER.
NOW!
ZZZAP!
QUI'EN GAIA FAE'LRA!

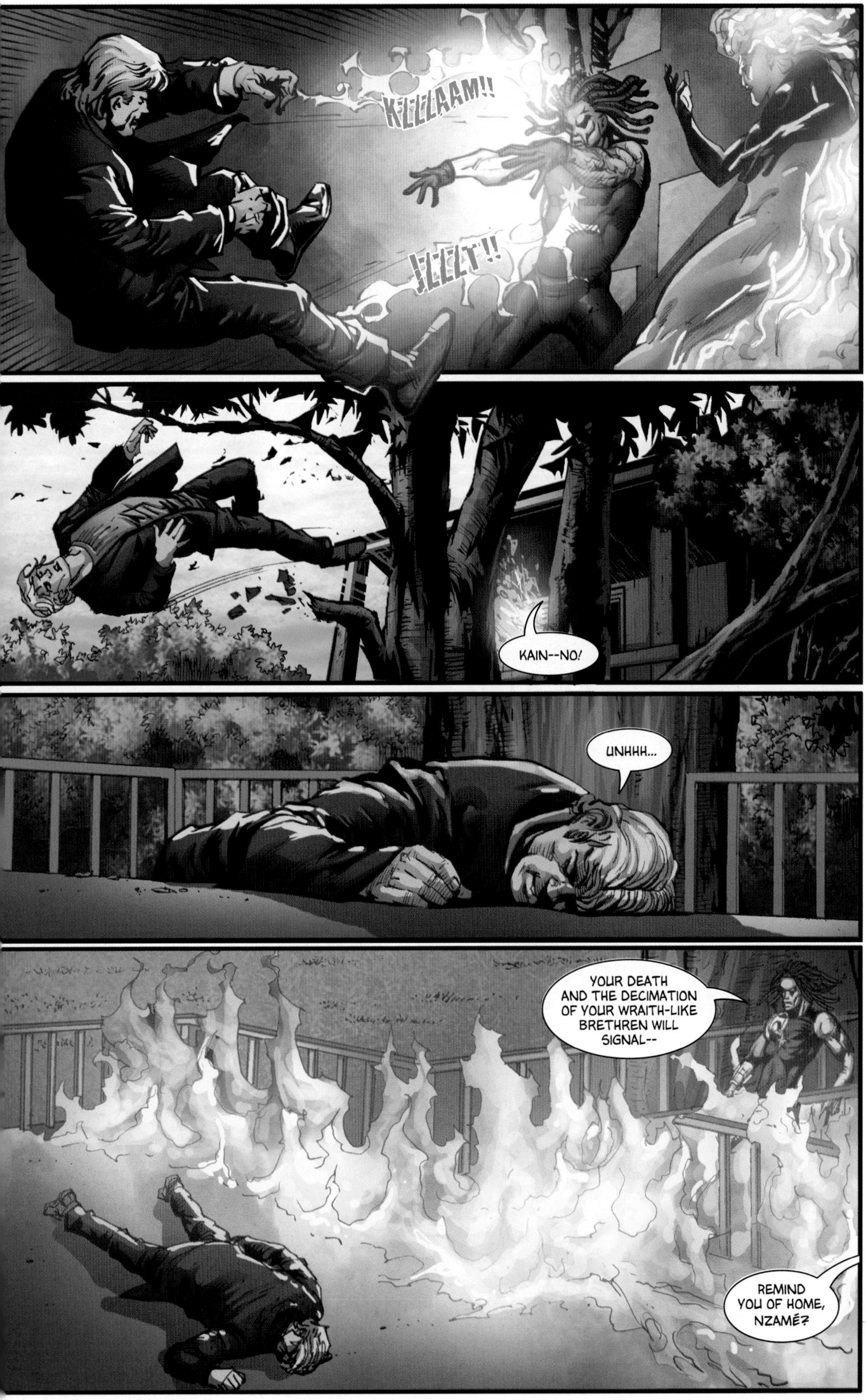
KLLLZAAM!!
ZZZZT!!
KAIN--NO!
UNHHH...
YOUR DEATH AND THE DECIMATION OF YOUR WRAITH-LIKE BRETHREN WILL SIGNAL--
REMIND YOU OF HOME, NZAMÉ?

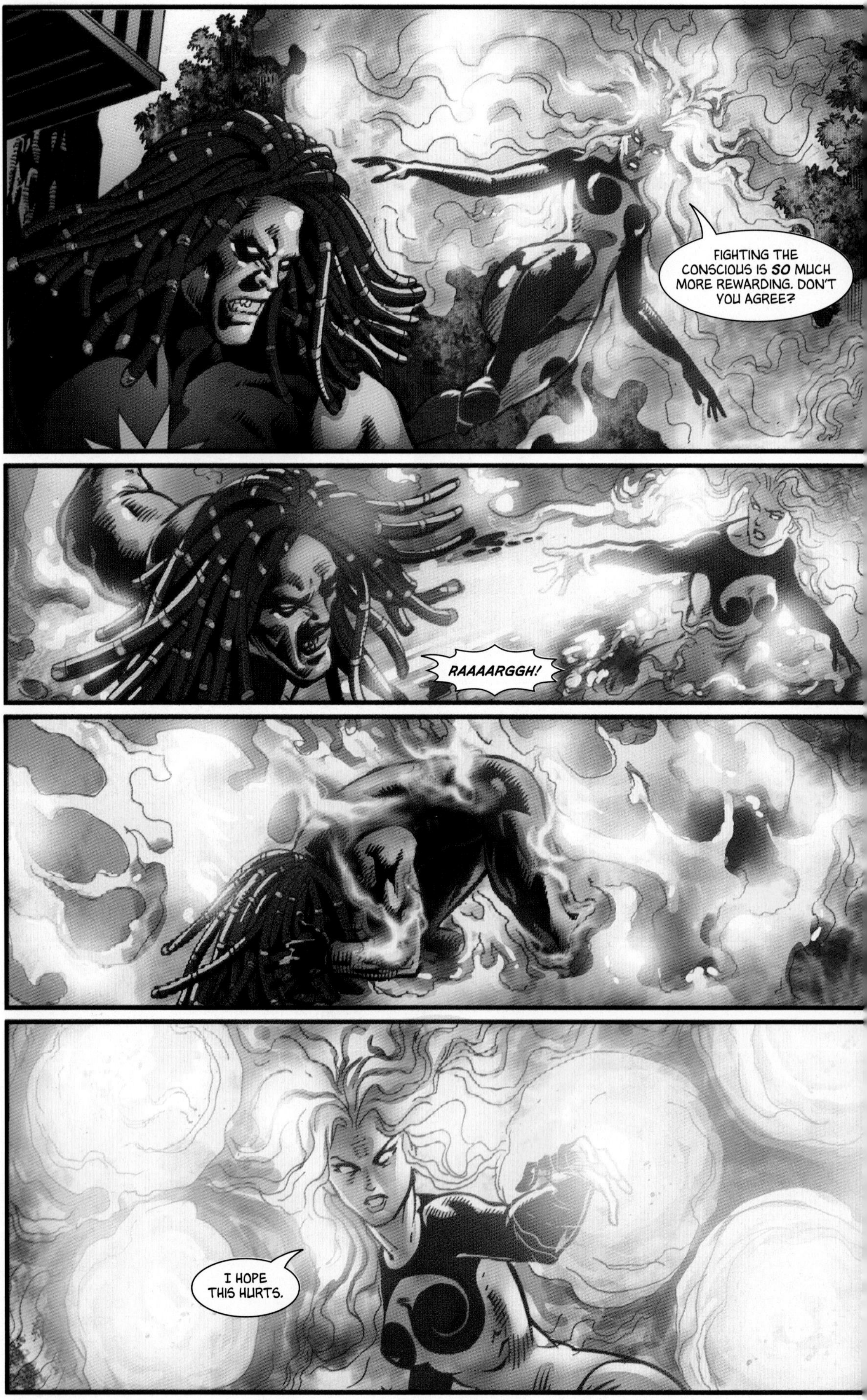
FIGHTING THE CONSCIOUS IS SO MUCH MORE REWARDING. DON'T YOU AGREE?
RAAAARGGH!
I HOPE THIS HURTS.

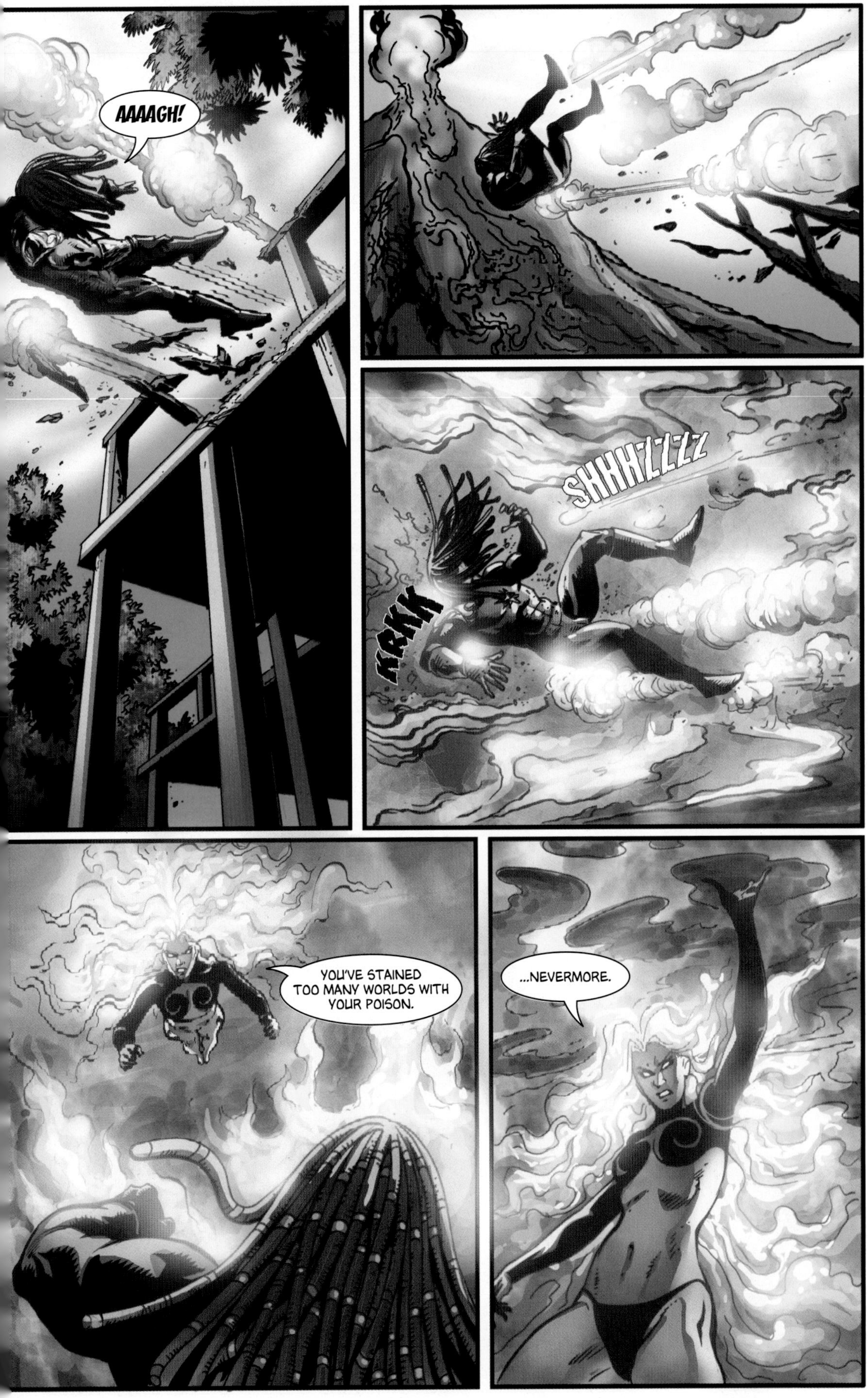
AAAAGH!
SHHHZZZZ
KRKK
YOU'VE STAINED TOO MANY WORLDS WITH YOUR POISON.
...NEVERMORE.

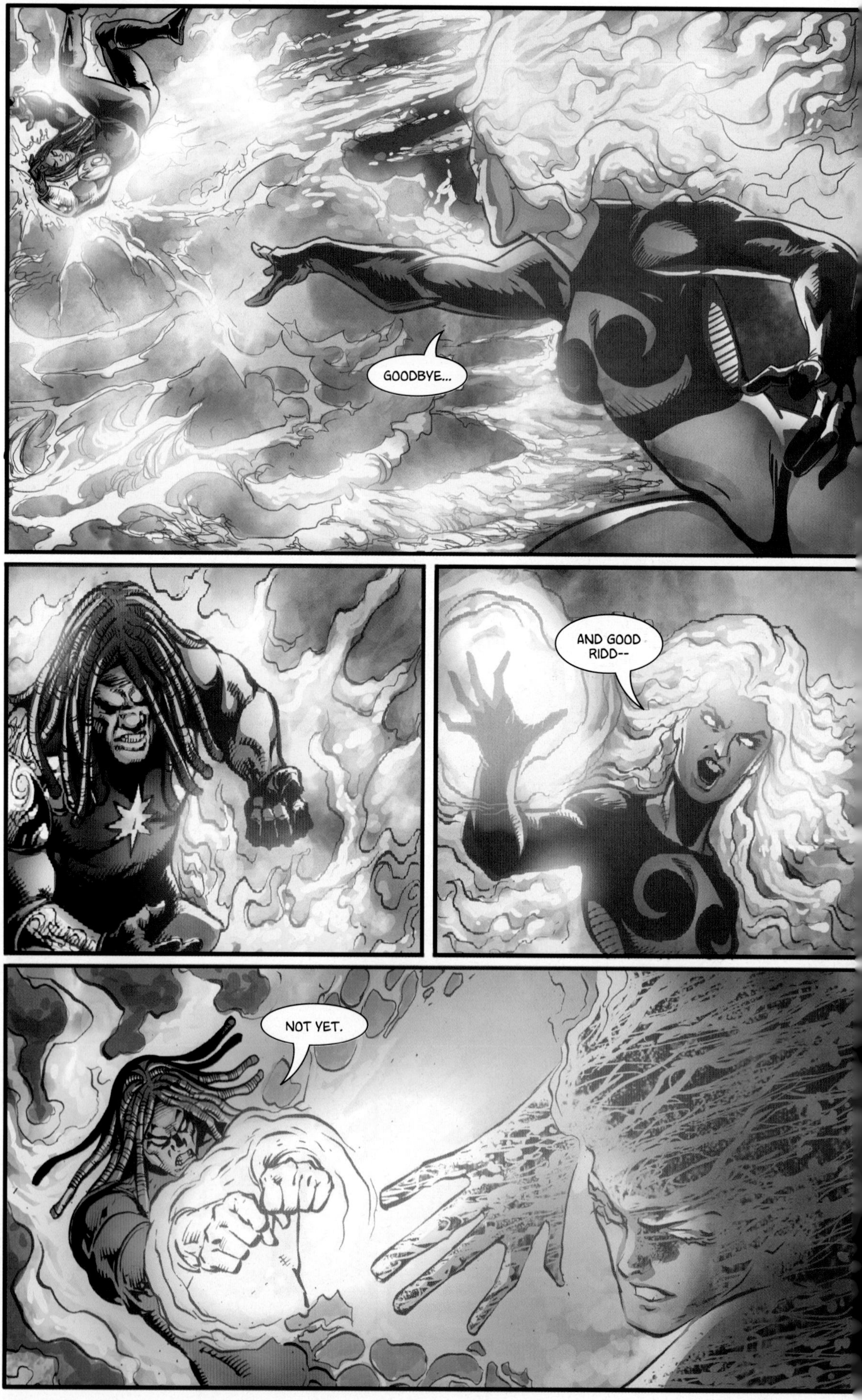
GOODBYE...
AND GOOD RIDD--
NOT YET.

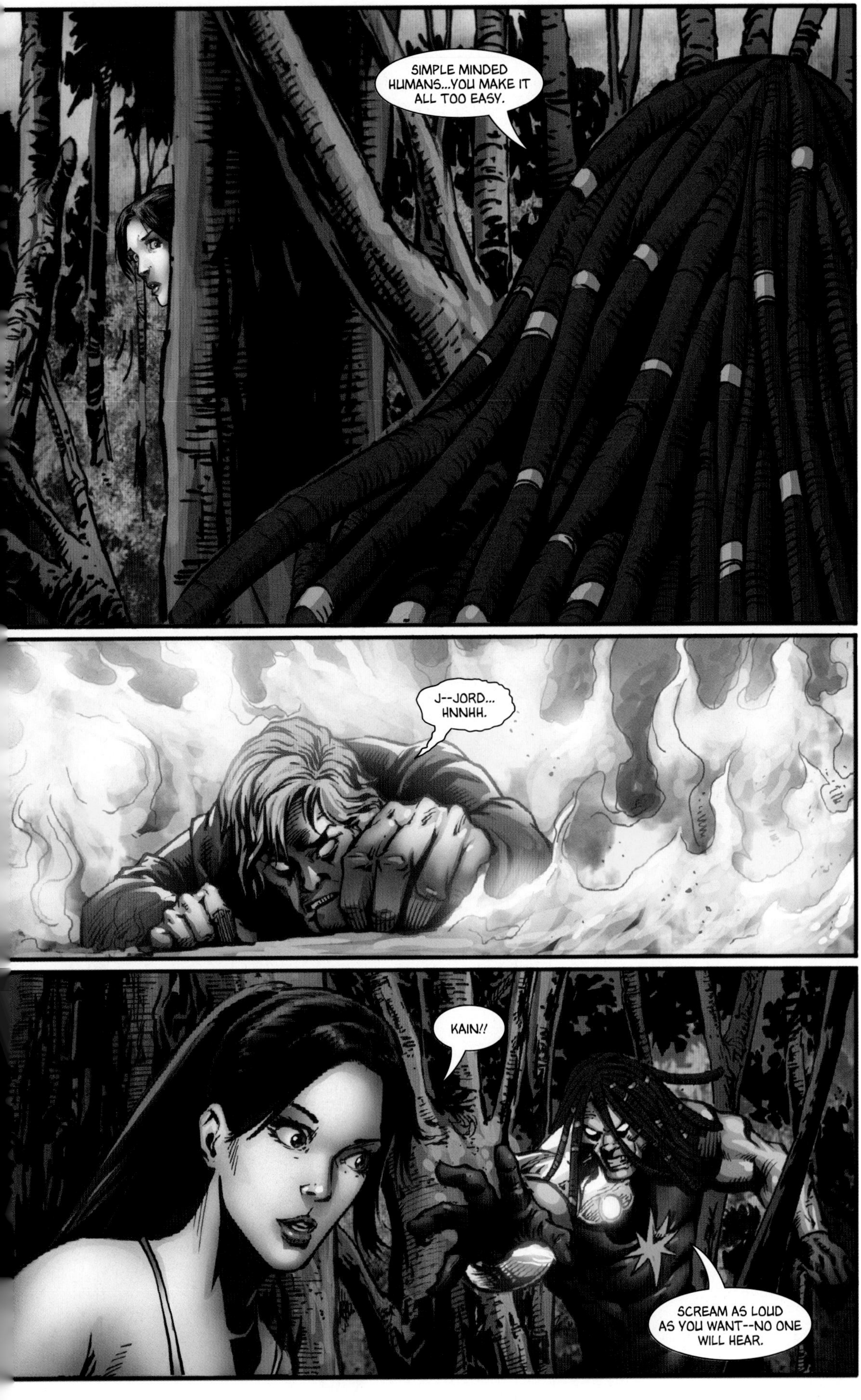
SIMPLE MINDED HUMANS...YOU MAKE IT ALL TOO EASY.
J--JORD... HNNHH.
KAIN!!
SCREAM AS LOUD AS YOU WANT--NO ONE WILL HEAR.

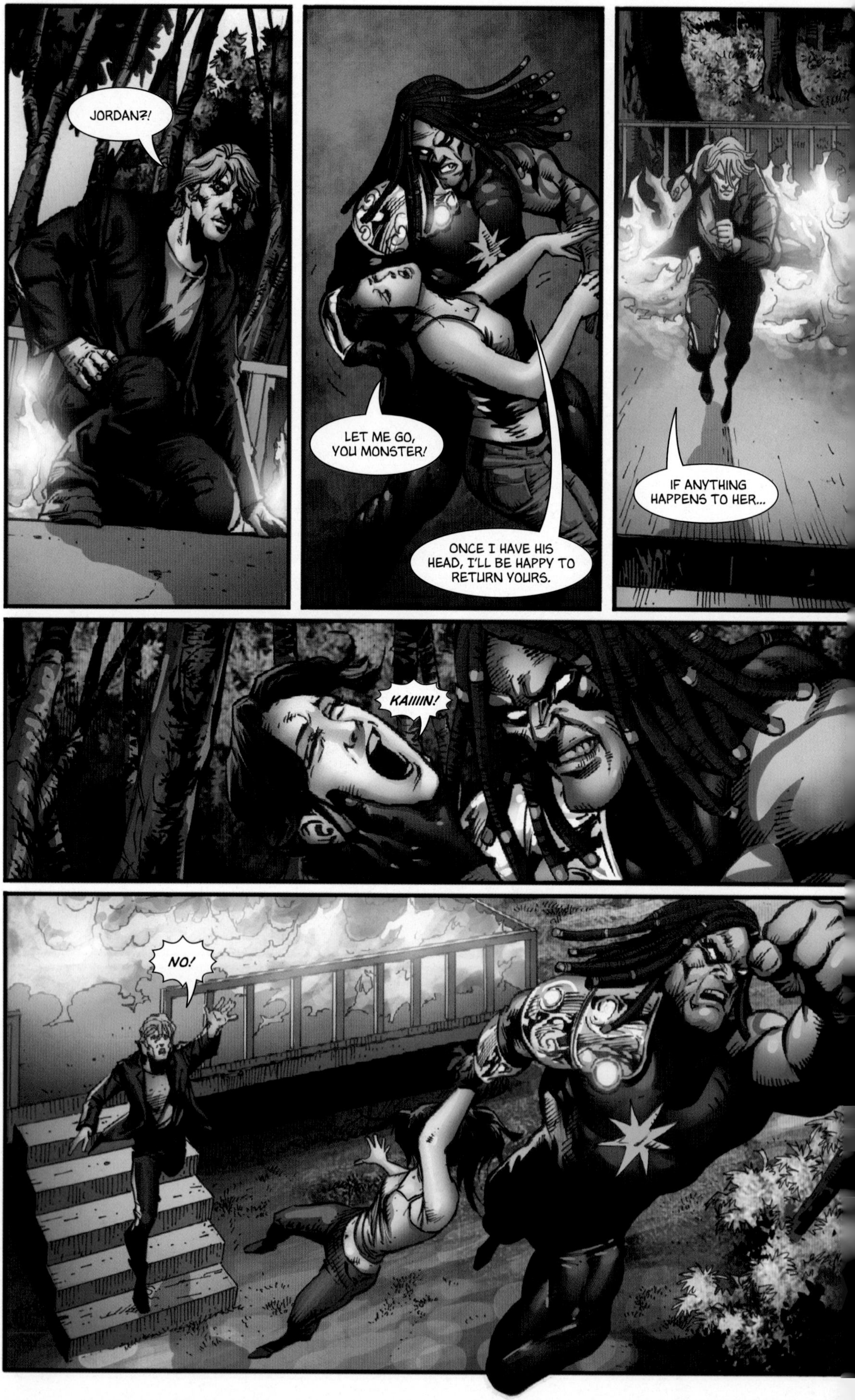
JORDAN?!
LET ME GO, YOU MONSTER!
ONCE I HAVE HIS HEAD, I'LL BE HAPPY TO RETURN YOURS.
IF ANYTHING HAPPENS TO HER...
KAIIIIN!
NO!

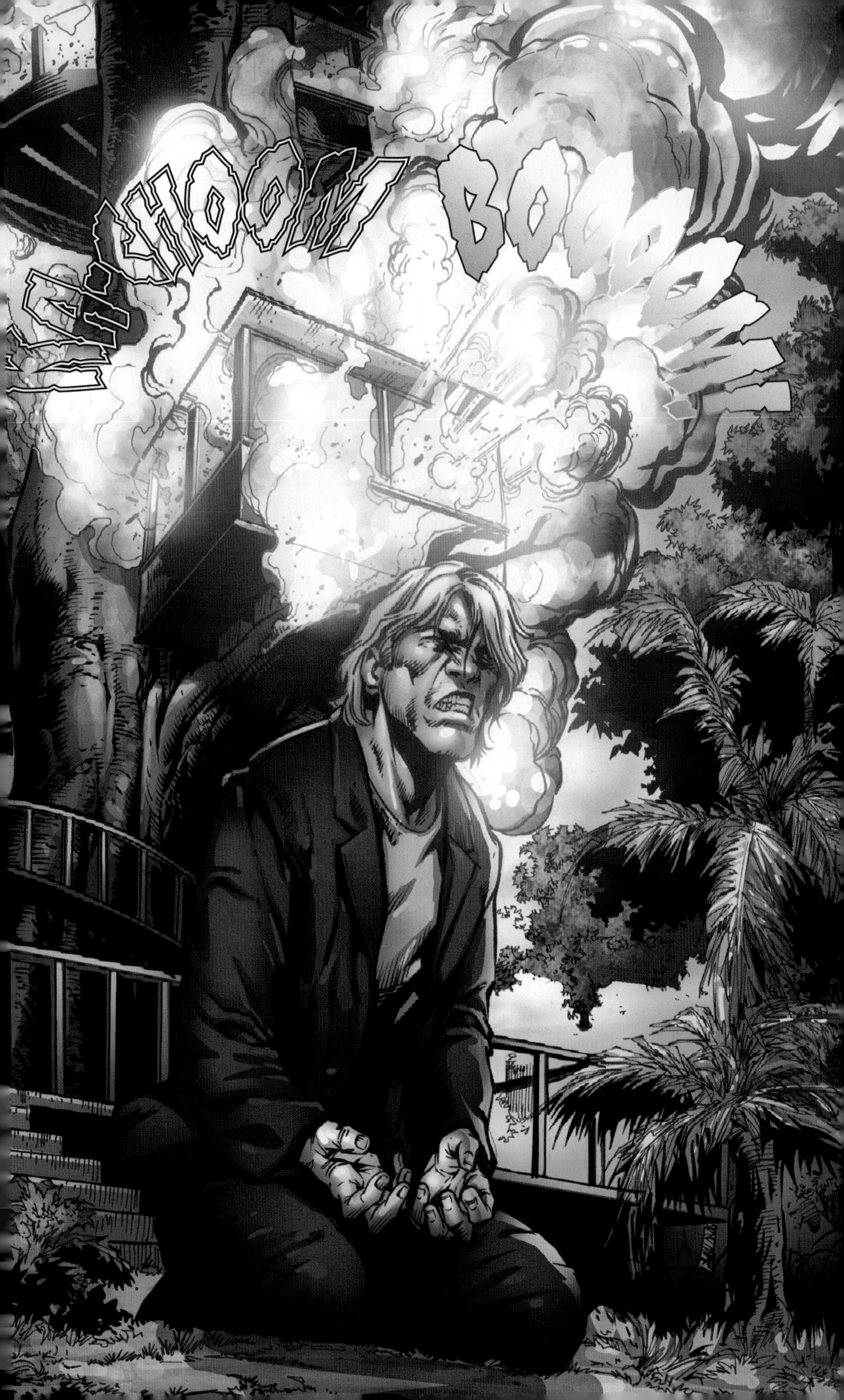
WHHOOM
BOOOOM!

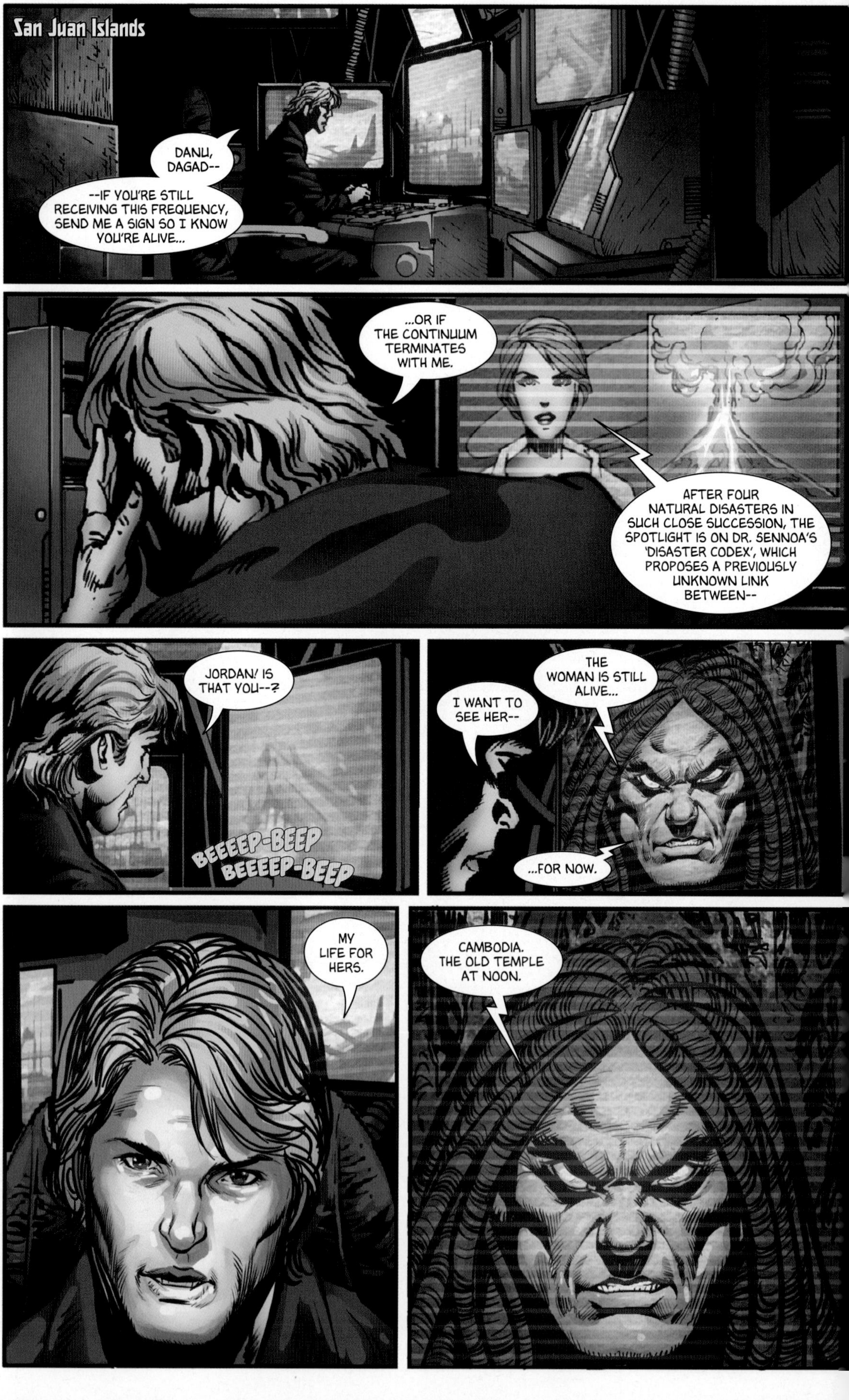
San Juan Islands
DANU, DAGAD--
--IF YOU'RE STILL RECEIVING THIS FREQUENCY, SEND ME A SIGN SO I KNOW YOU'RE ALIVE...
...OR IF THE CONTINUUM TERMINATES WITH ME.
AFTER FOUR NATURAL DISASTERS IN SUCH CLOSE SUCCESSION, THE SPOTLIGHT IS ON DR. SENNOA'S 'DISASTER CODEX', WHICH PROPOSES A PREVIOUSLY UNKNOWN LINK BETWEEN--
JORDAN! IS THAT YOU--?
BEEEEP-BEEP
BEEEEP-BEEP
THE WOMAN IS STILL ALIVE...
I WANT TO SEE HER--
...FOR NOW.
MY LIFE FOR HERS.
CAMBODIA. THE OLD TEMPLE AT NOON.

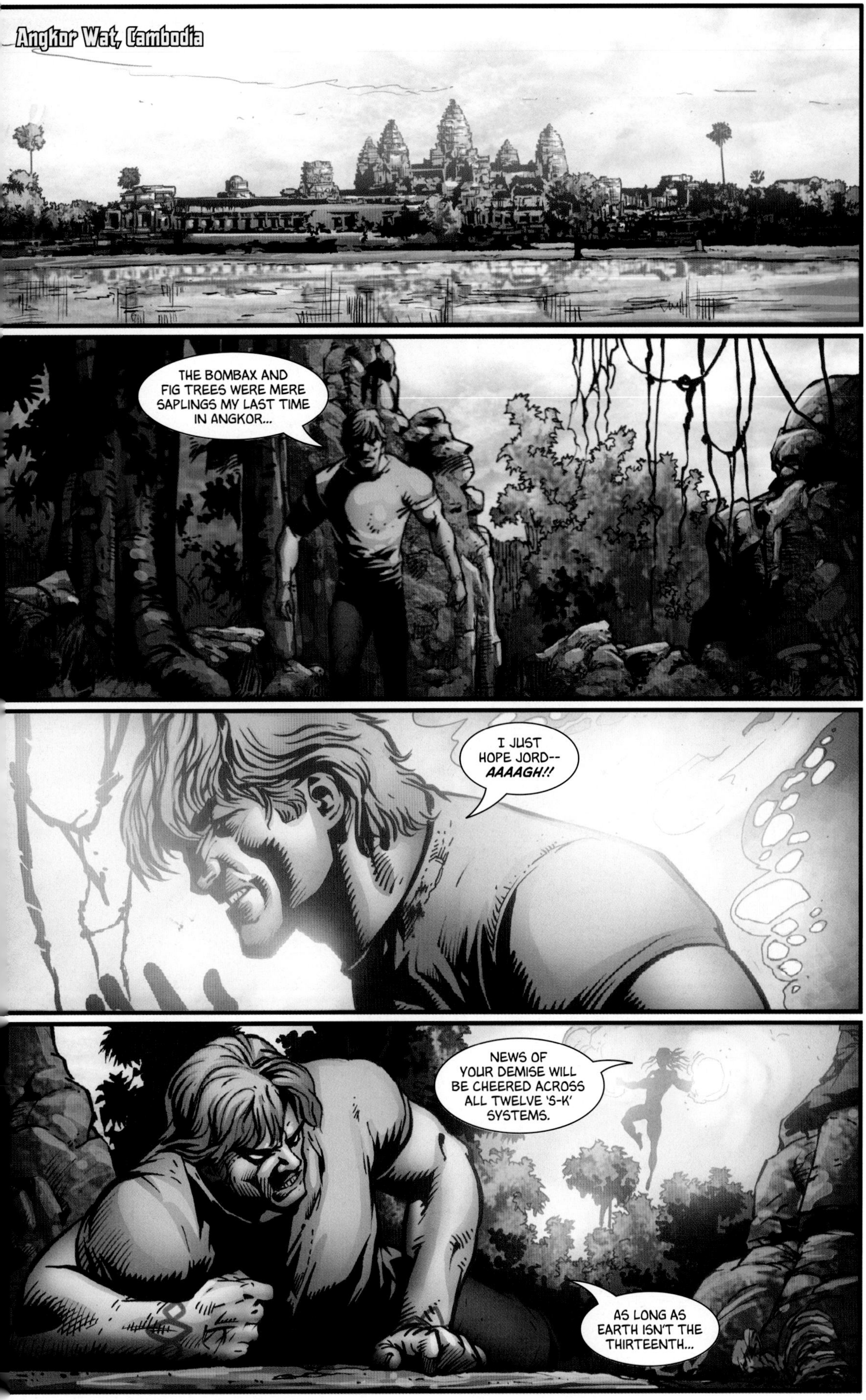

Angkor Wat, Cambodia
THE BOMBAX AND FIG TREES WERE MERE SAPLINGS MY LAST TIME IN ANGKOR...
I JUST HOPE JORD-- *AAAAGH!!*
NEWS OF YOUR DEMISE WILL BE CHEERED ACROSS ALL TWELVE 'S-K' SYSTEMS.
AS LONG AS EARTH ISN'T THE THIRTEENTH...

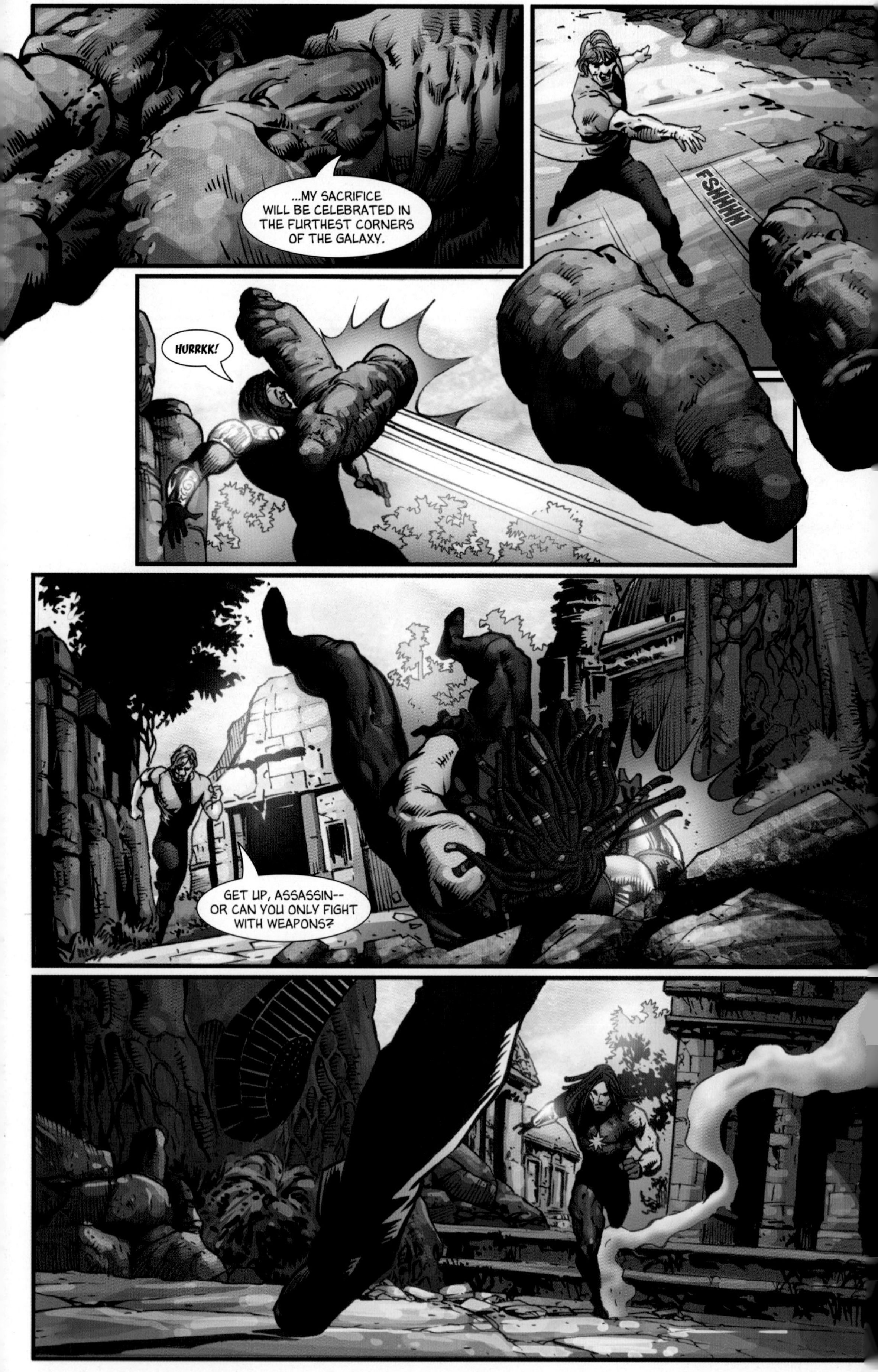
...MY SACRIFICE WILL BE CELEBRATED IN THE FURTHEST CORNERS OF THE GALAXY.
FSHHHH
HURRKK!
GET UP, ASSASSIN-- OR CAN YOU ONLY FIGHT WITH WEAPONS?

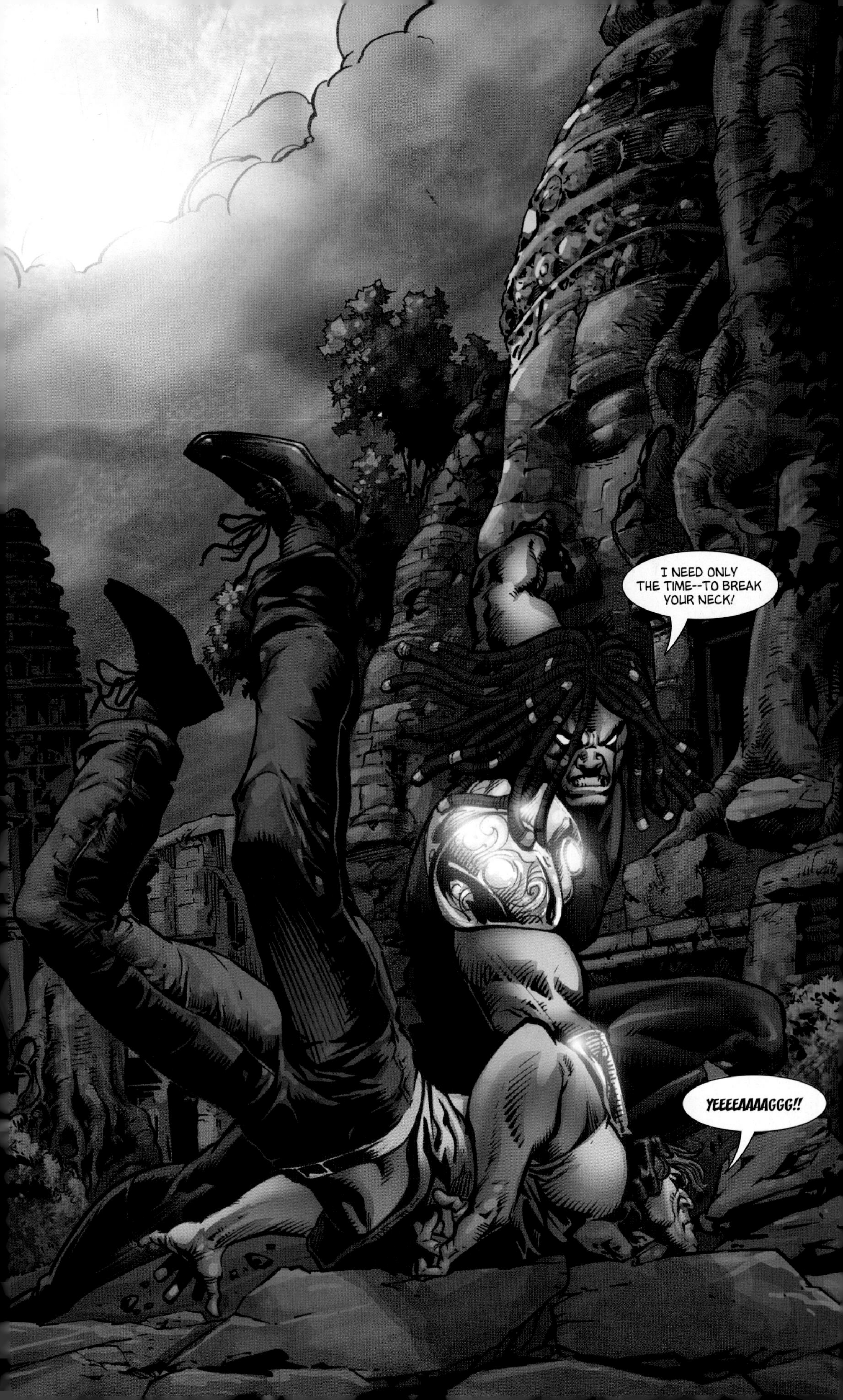
I NEED ONLY THE TIME--TO BREAK YOUR NECK!
YEEEEAAAAGGG!!

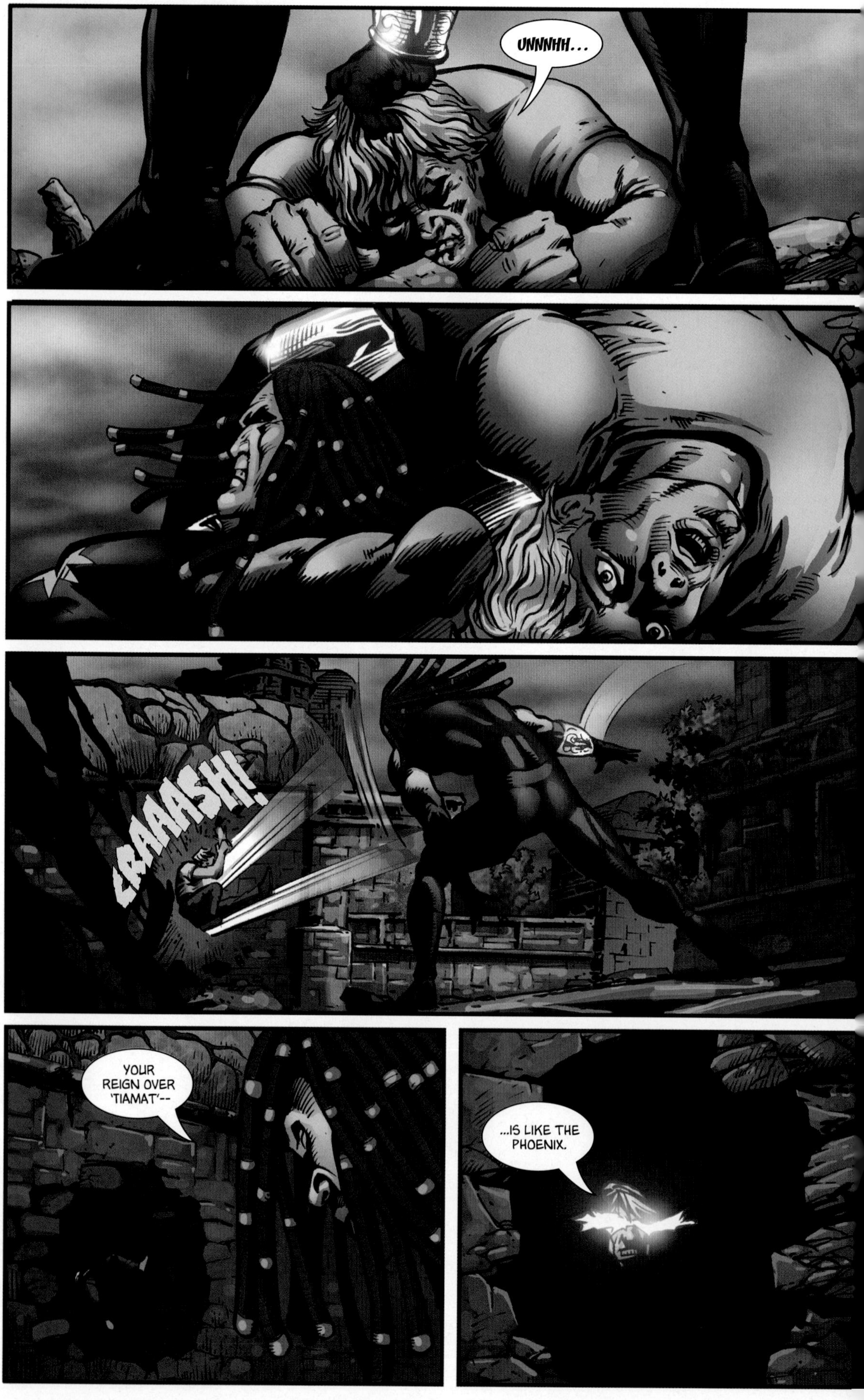
UNNNHH...
CRAAASH!!
YOUR REIGN OVER 'TIAMAT'--
...IS LIKE THE PHOENIX.

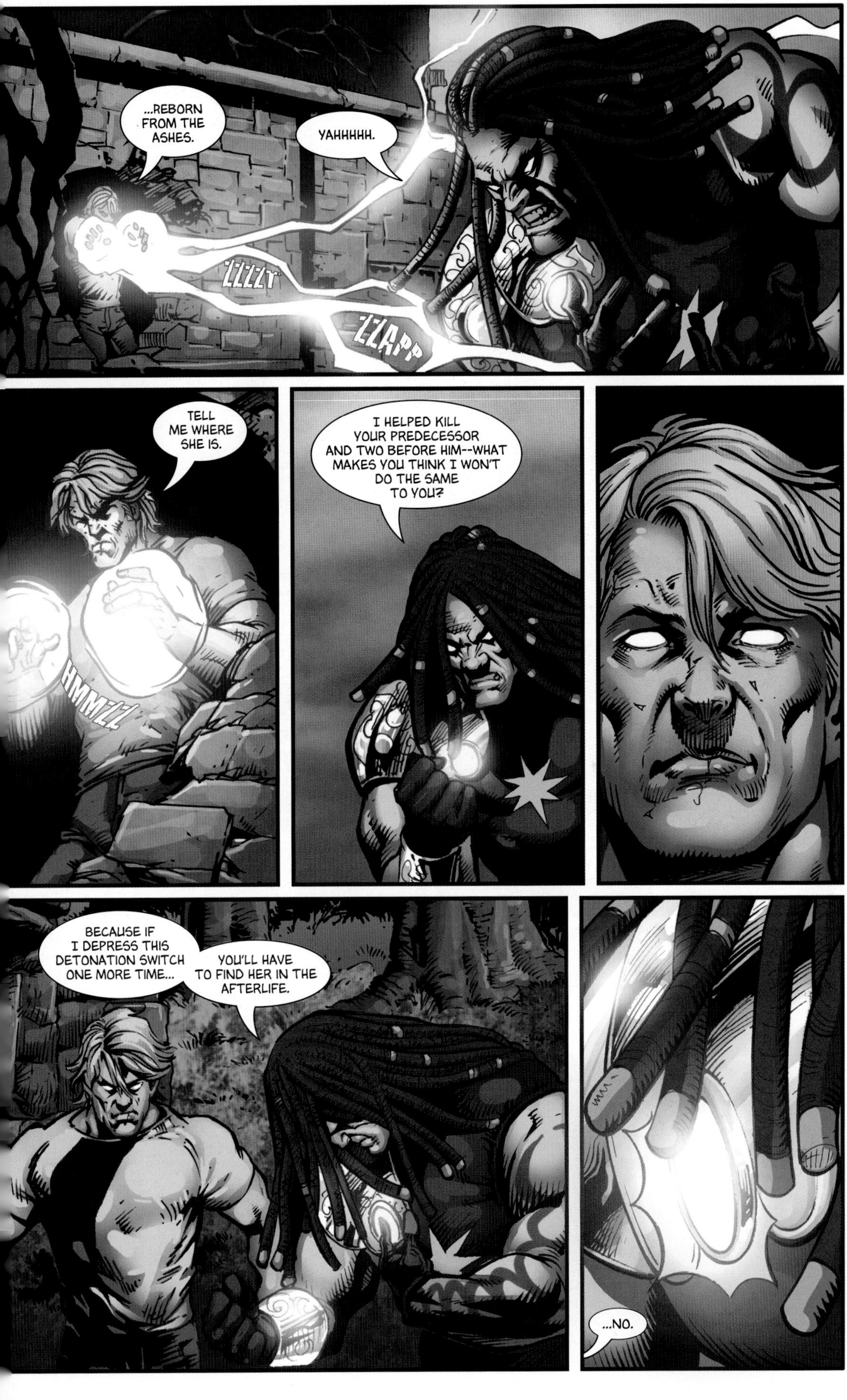
...REBORN FROM THE ASHES.
YAHHHHH.
ZZZZT
ZZAPP
TELL ME WHERE SHE IS.
HMMZZ
I HELPED KILL YOUR PREDECESSOR AND TWO BEFORE HIM--WHAT MAKES YOU THINK I WON'T DO THE SAME TO YOU?
BECAUSE IF I DEPRESS THIS DETONATION SWITCH ONE MORE TIME...
YOU'LL HAVE TO FIND HER IN THE AFTERLIFE.
...NO.

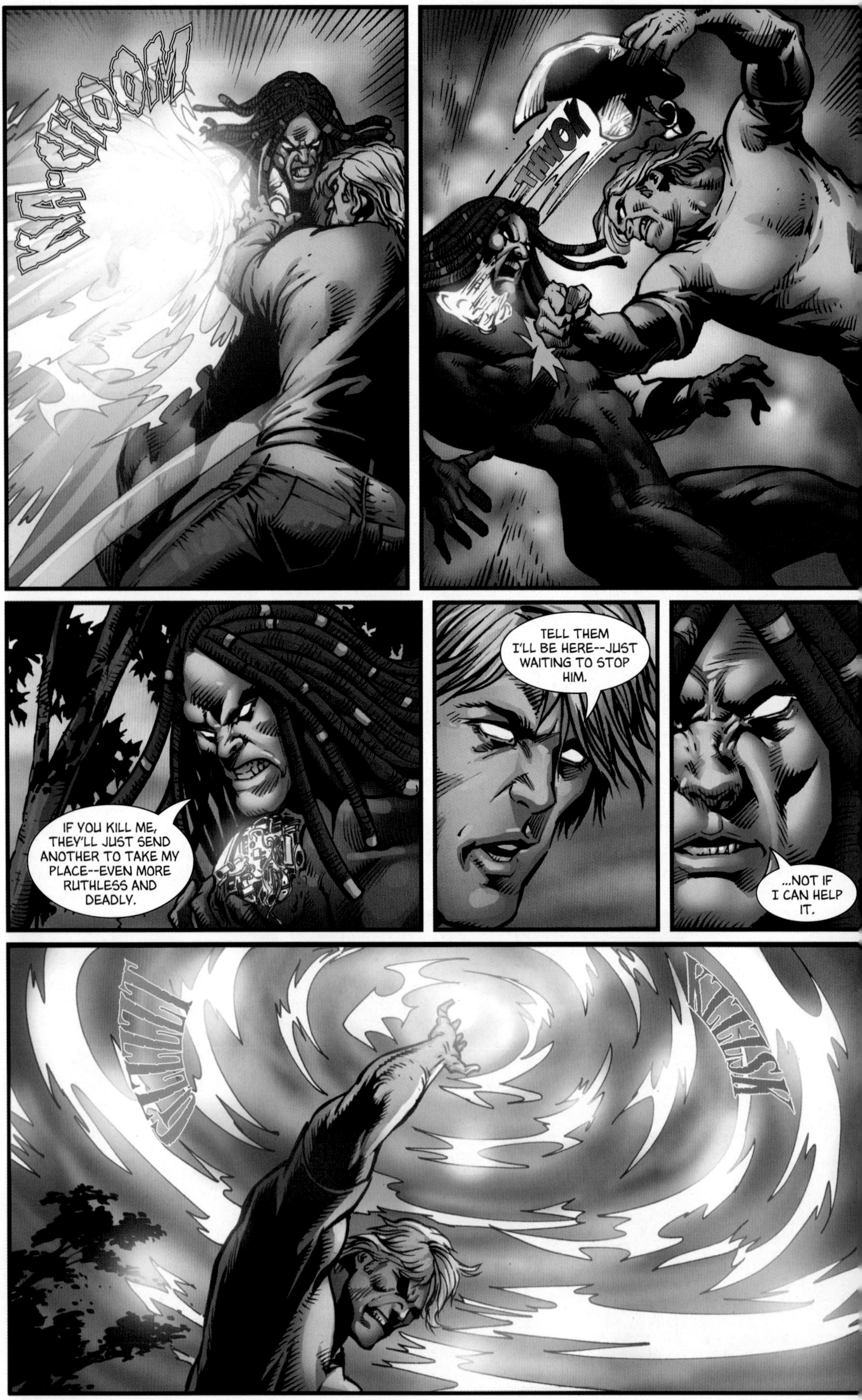
WA-CHOOM
IOWW!!
IF YOU KILL ME, THEY'LL JUST SEND ANOTHER TO TAKE MY PLACE--EVEN MORE RUTHLESS AND DEADLY.
TELL THEM I'LL BE HERE--JUST WAITING TO STOP HIM.
...NOT IF I CAN HELP IT.

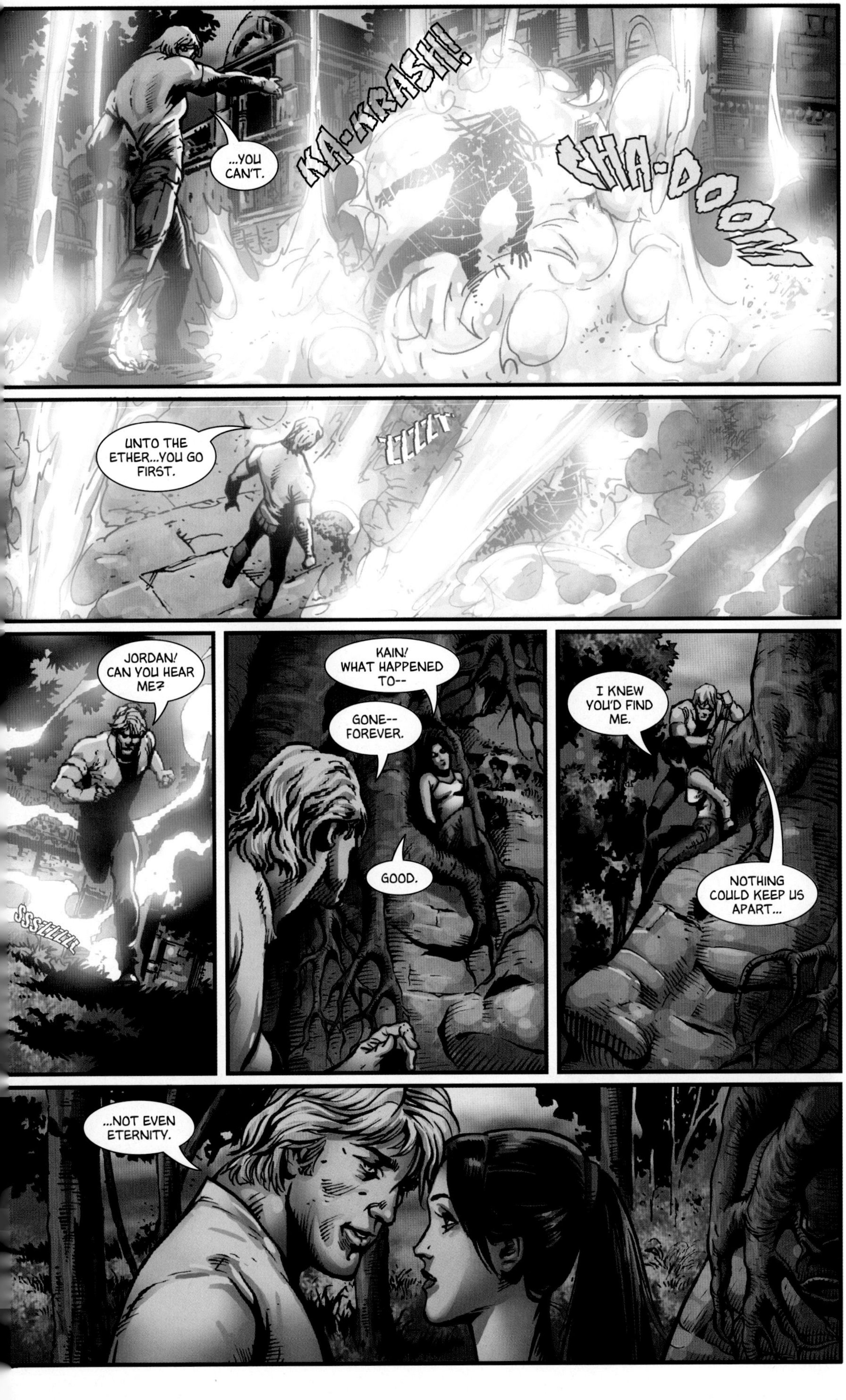

...YOU CAN'T.
KA-KRASH!!
THA-DOOM
UNTO THE ETHER...YOU GO FIRST.
ZZZZT
JORDAN! CAN YOU HEAR ME?
SSSZZZZZ
KAIN! WHAT HAPPENED TO--
GONE-- FOREVER.
GOOD.
I KNEW YOU'D FIND ME.
NOTHING COULD KEEP US APART...
...NOT EVEN ETERNITY.

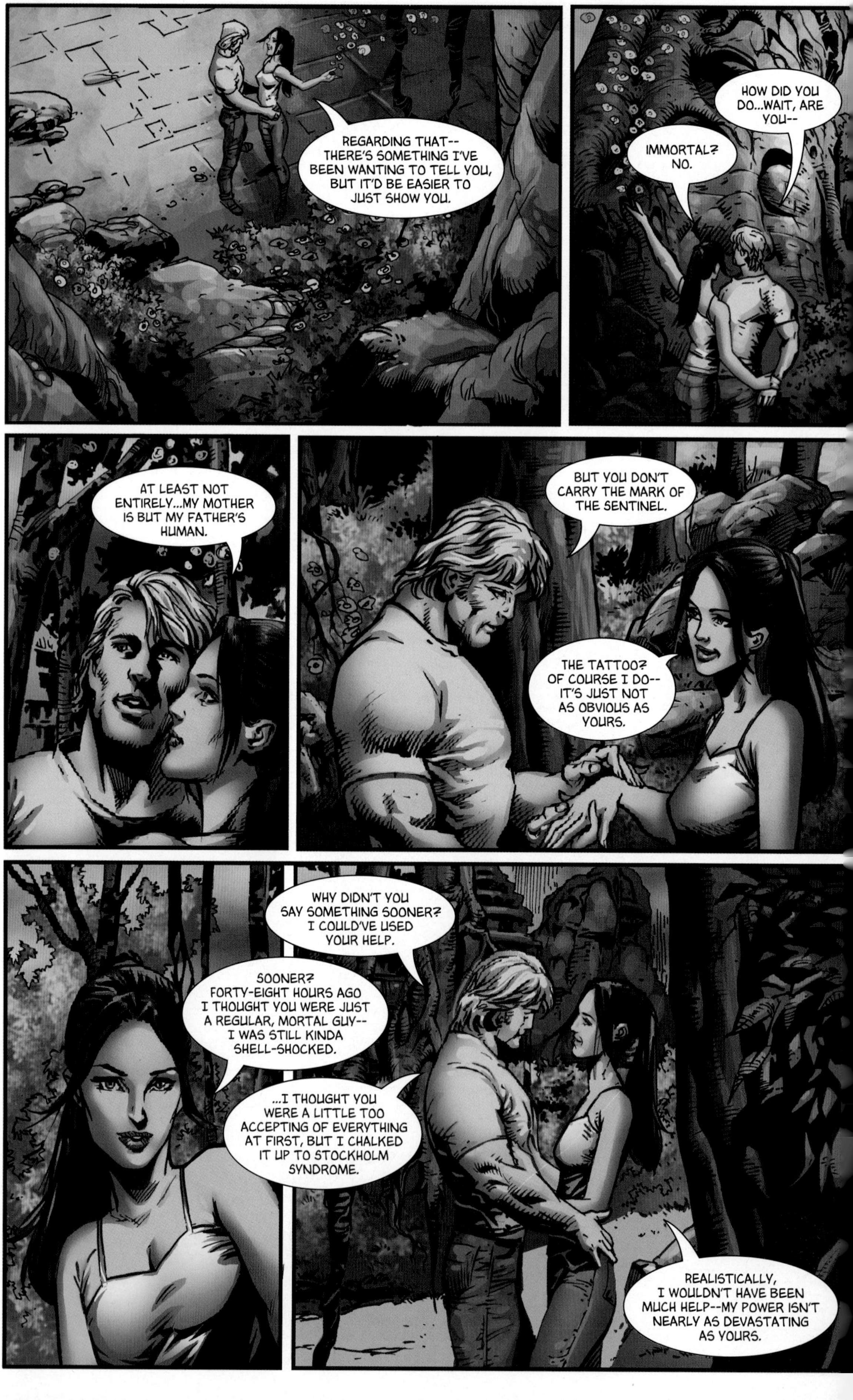
REGARDING THAT-- THERE'S SOMETHING I'VE BEEN WANTING TO TELL YOU, BUT IT'D BE EASIER TO JUST SHOW YOU.
HOW DID YOU DO...WAIT, ARE YOU--
IMMORTAL? NO.
AT LEAST NOT ENTIRELY...MY MOTHER IS BUT MY FATHER'S HUMAN.
BUT YOU DON'T CARRY THE MARK OF THE SENTINEL.
THE TATTOO? OF COURSE I DO-- IT'S JUST NOT AS OBVIOUS AS YOURS.
WHY DIDN'T YOU SAY SOMETHING SOONER? I COULD'VE USED YOUR HELP.
SOONER? FORTY-EIGHT HOURS AGO I THOUGHT YOU WERE JUST A REGULAR, MORTAL GUY-- I WAS STILL KINDA SHELL-SHOCKED.
...I THOUGHT YOU WERE A LITTLE TOO ACCEPTING OF EVERYTHING AT FIRST, BUT I CHALKED IT UP TO STOCKHOLM SYNDROME.
REALISTICALLY, I WOULDN'T HAVE BEEN MUCH HELP--MY POWER ISN'T NEARLY AS DEVASTATING AS YOURS.

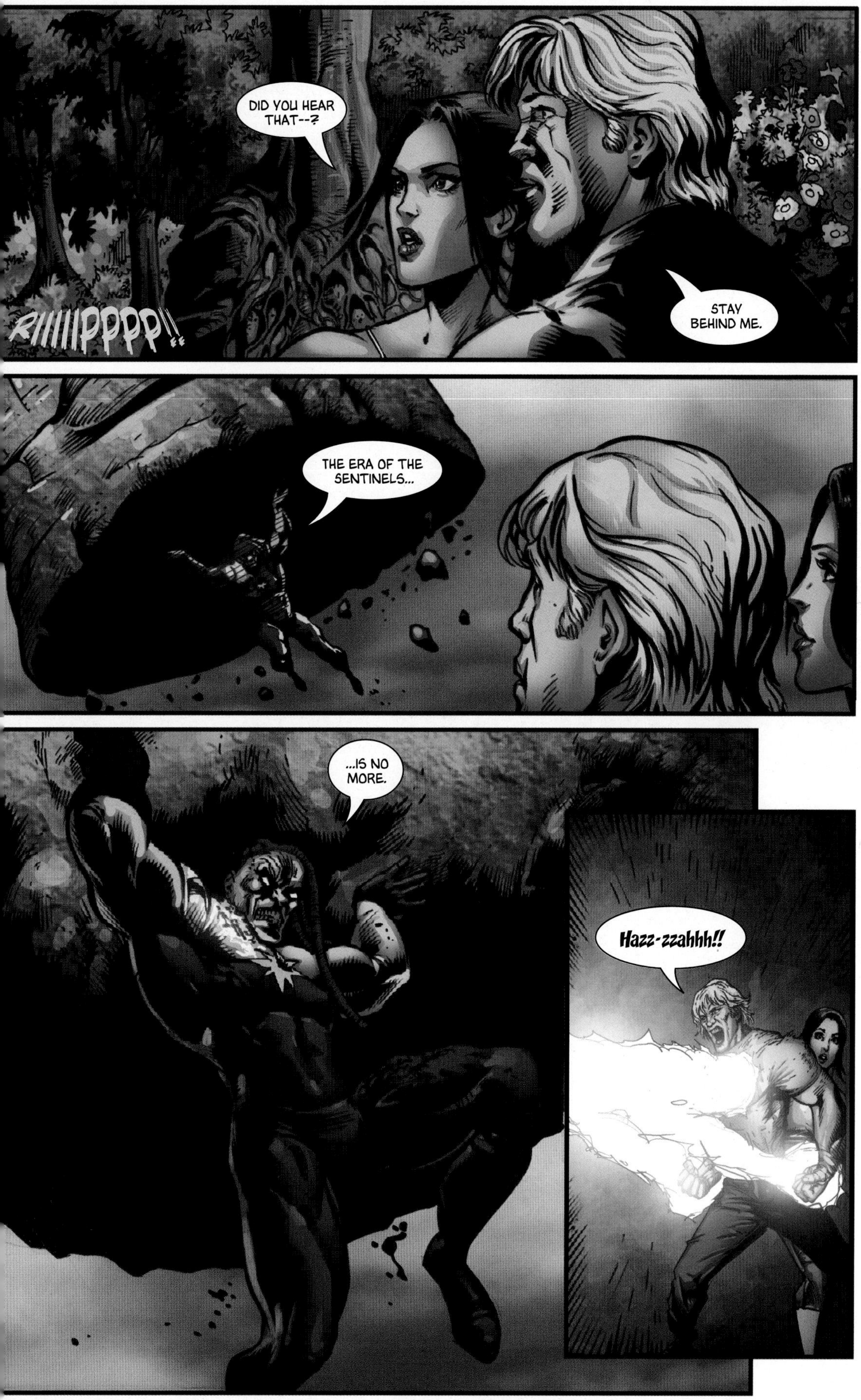
DID YOU HEAR THAT--?
STAY BEHIND ME.
RIIIIIPPPP!!
THE ERA OF THE SENTINELS...
...IS NO MORE.
Hazz-zzahhh!!

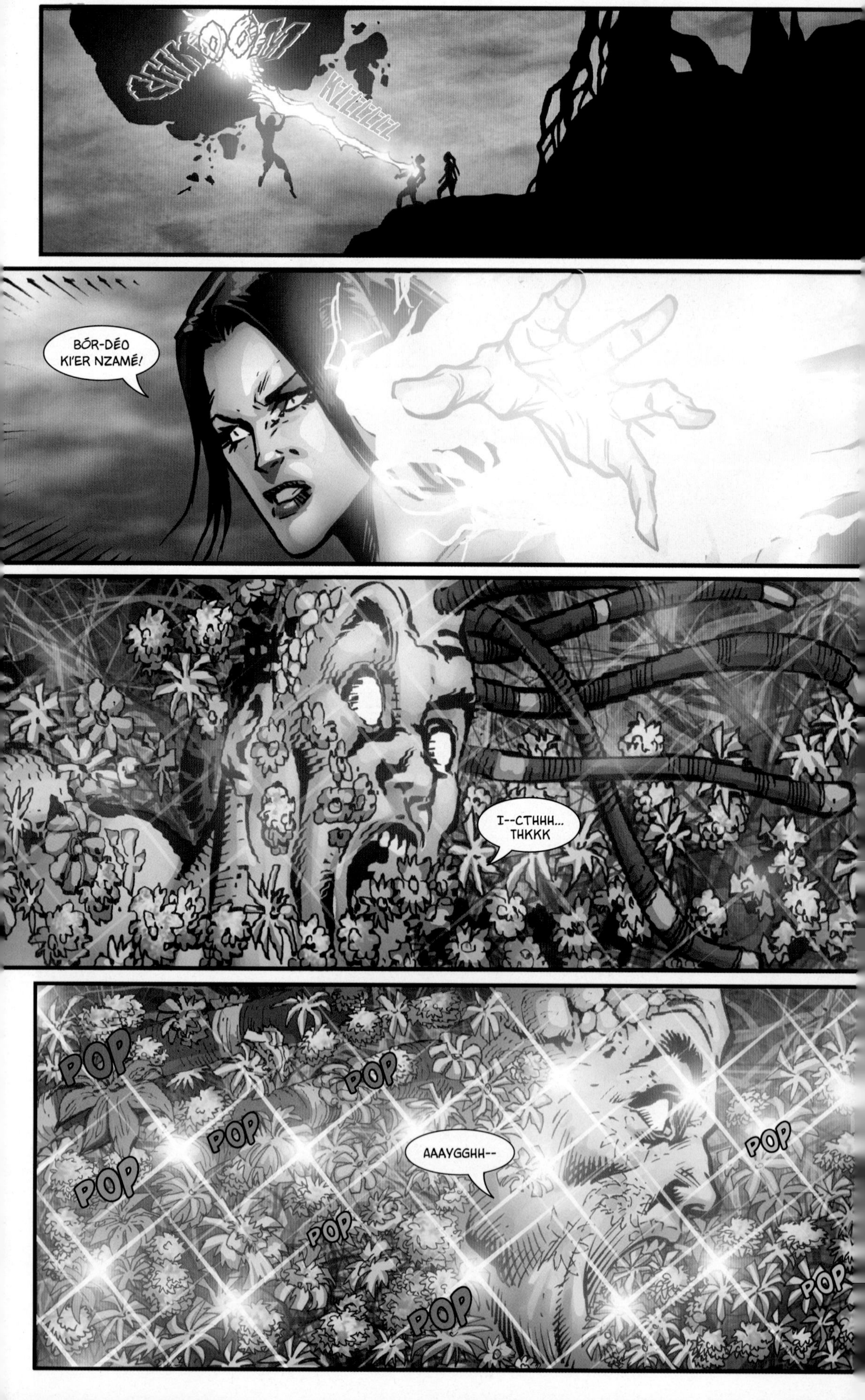
BÓR-DÉO
KI'ER NZAMÉ!
I--CTHHH...
THKKK
POP
POP
POP
POP
AAAYGGHH--
POP
POP
POP
POP

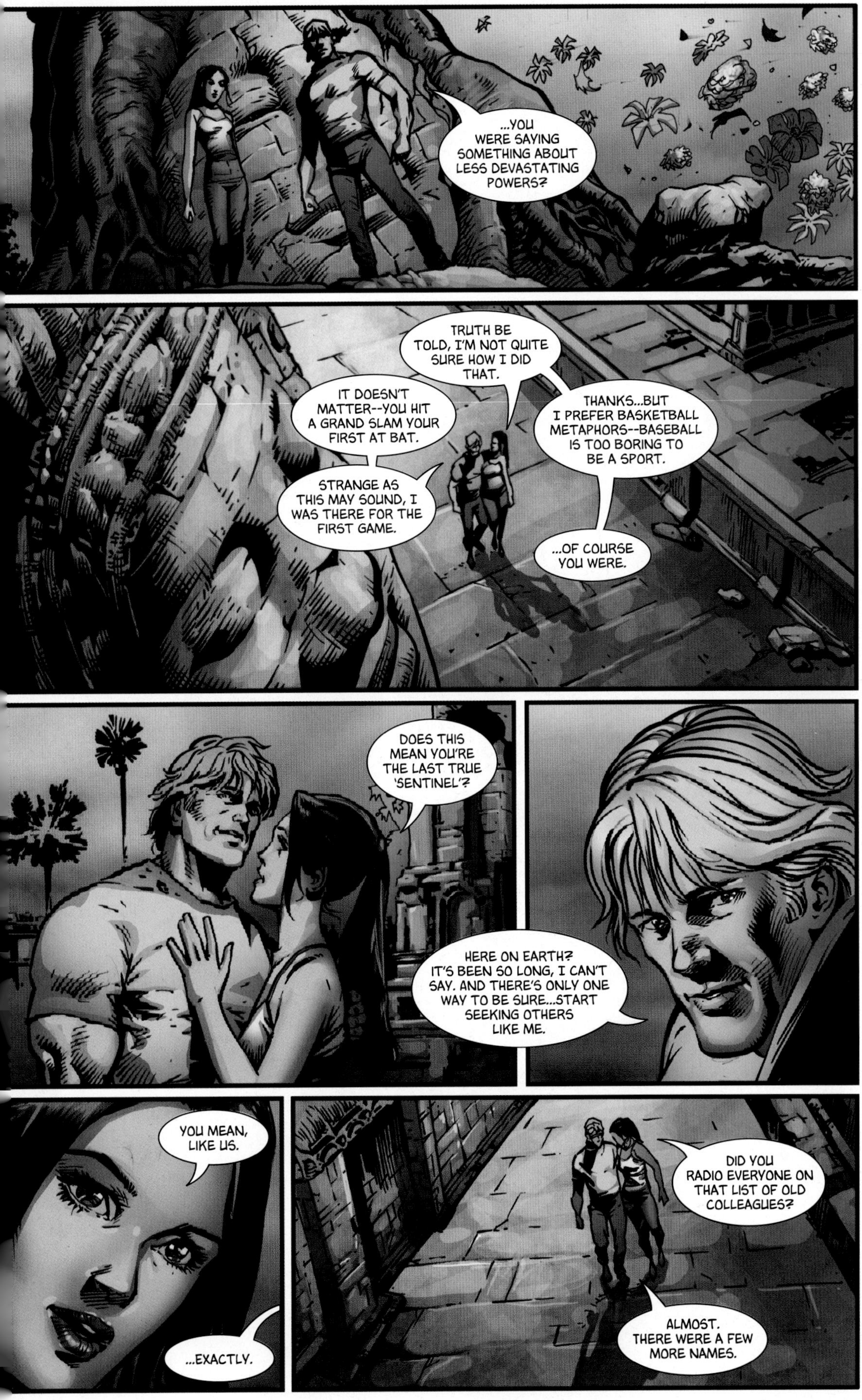
...YOU WERE SAYING SOMETHING ABOUT LESS DEVASTATING POWERS?
TRUTH BE TOLD, I'M NOT QUITE SURE HOW I DID THAT.
IT DOESN'T MATTER--YOU HIT A GRAND SLAM YOUR FIRST AT BAT.
THANKS...BUT I PREFER BASKETBALL METAPHORS--BASEBALL IS TOO BORING TO BE A SPORT.
STRANGE AS THIS MAY SOUND, I WAS THERE FOR THE FIRST GAME.
...OF COURSE YOU WERE.
DOES THIS MEAN YOU'RE THE LAST TRUE 'SENTINEL'?
HERE ON EARTH? IT'S BEEN SO LONG, I CAN'T SAY. AND THERE'S ONLY ONE WAY TO BE SURE...START SEEKING OTHERS LIKE ME.
YOU MEAN, LIKE US.
...EXACTLY.
DID YOU RADIO EVERYONE ON THAT LIST OF OLD COLLEAGUES?
ALMOST. THERE WERE A FEW MORE NAMES.

AREN'T YOU THE LEAST BIT CURIOUS? I MEAN I'D BE HAPPY TO HELP.

YOU'RE NOT TOO BUSY?

SUDDENLY, I'VE GOT ALL THE TIME IN THE WORLD.

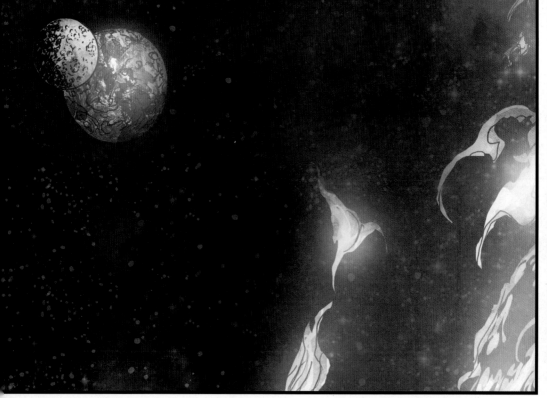

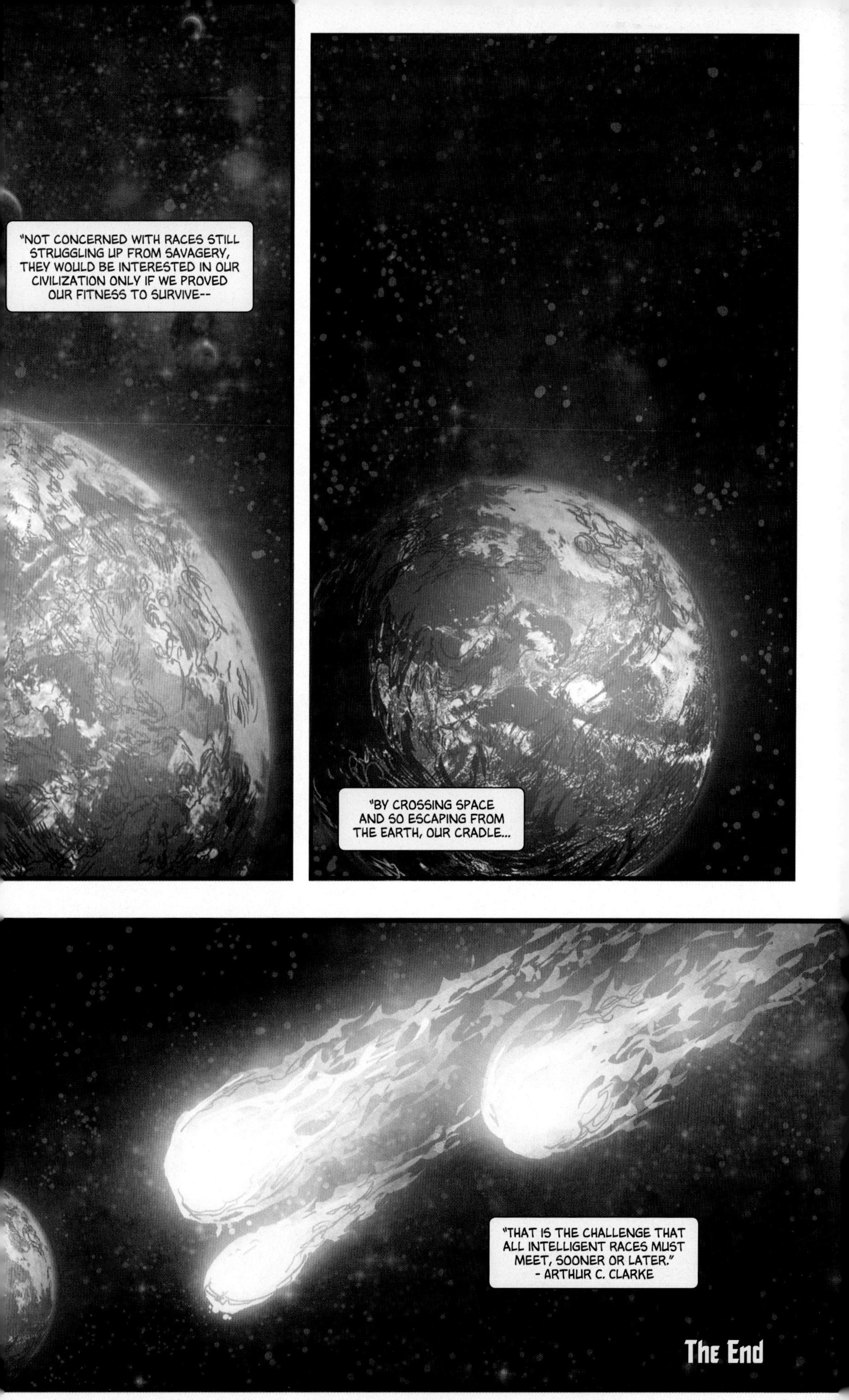
"NOT CONCERNED WITH RACES STILL STRUGGLING UP FROM SAVAGERY, THEY WOULD BE INTERESTED IN OUR CIVILIZATION ONLY IF WE PROVED OUR FITNESS TO SURVIVE--
"BY CROSSING SPACE AND SO ESCAPING FROM THE EARTH, OUR CRADLE...
"THAT IS THE CHALLENGE THAT ALL INTELLIGENT RACES MUST MEET, SOONER OR LATER." - ARTHUR C. CLARKE
The End